MW00583646

endorsements

"A deeply moving and clear-eyed memoir filled with poetry, art and most of all — love."

—**Jacqueline Woodson** - Former Library of Congress National Ambassador for Young People's Literature; Astrid Lindgren Memorial Award Laureate 2018; Author of *Brown Girl Dreaming* - National Book Award Winner 2014; Author of *Another Brooklyn* - National Book Award Finalist 2016; Author of *Red at the Bone* (Riverhead, 2019)

"*Growing Up Ugly* is a coming-of-age story that represents those most often unheard and unseen. At the heart of Rolling's memoir is the weaving together of multiple creative modes of expression to invite in adolescent readers and to share stories with language, prose, and illustrations that will resonate with generations to come. This book should especially be introduced to male readers of color whose identities and experiences are least represented in the field of children's and adolescent literature. *Growing Up Ugly* signals a turn toward more honest and authentic first-person accounts of the Black male experience in America."

—**Dr. Marcelle Haddix** - Professor of Literacy, Syracuse University; 2019 President, Literacy Research Association

"Once again the United States is being called upon to take an unflinching look at what it means to be Black in America. James Rolling has given us a gift; an honest account of his own experience. Told in vignettes, photos, and original poetry, *Growing Up Ugly* reveals the struggle with self-image and discovery of purpose that marks every human life, but is particularly acute for men of color. While the narrative of the African diaspora on this continent remains unfinished, this poignant memoir adds to our collective journey toward understanding and healing."

—**Rev. John Carter** - Lead Pastor, Abundant Life, Syracuse, NY; Author of *The Transformed Life* (Harrison House, 2014)

"Rooted in poignant personal experiences, Rolling's unflinching narrative and evocative poems shed compelling insights into youth anxieties through the lens of his own struggles with identity, appearance, friendships, and a lifetime of racialized spaces and encounters. Candidly sharing a series of short vignettes ranging from bouts with asthma, bullying, abuse, a father's flaws, and shattered dreams, this memoir is ultimately a tale of transcendence as an ugly duckling becomes a swan. *Growing Up Ugly* is a transformative journey for every adolescent, parent, and educator."

—**Dr. Uzo Unobagha** - ALA Notable Book Award-winning Author of *Off To The Sweet Shores of Africa and Other Talking Drum Rhymes*; Educator, Syracuse City School District, Syracuse, NY

"James Rolling has given the world the greatest of all gifts: HOPE, especially for those of us whose personal histories have left us marginalized, invisible, and without a healthy sense of self. Being the son of a Mohawk mother, I have found my face in Rolling's memoir, *Growing Up Ugly.* Yes, we have all been shaped by our personal histories. But we can all be more than those histories. Rolling's incredible book lights the way."

—**H. Dale Lloyd** - Author of *October's Dying: The Tragic Story of the North American Indigenous Peoples*

"In *Growing Up Ugly*, Dr. James H. Rolling, Jr. allows his readers a few precious moments inside the skin of a brilliant young man during his most formative years. We begin to grasp the complicated roots of his perceived ugliness. Yet from these roots, Rolling forges a network of circuitous routes toward identity formation. Along the way, he is challenged internally and externally by the onlooking gaze of a world that would dictate his value, his meaning, his very humanity, based on a constellation of factors that far exceed his own reach. Through his art and his intellect, our protagonist discovers a voice that has something to say to the world, and a beauty worth beholding. This book is all at once an excellent work of memoir, poetry, visual art, photography, and social commentary. What a privilege it is to see the world through the eyes of a child who doesn't know how beautiful he truly is! I know too many of them in my own life. I will share the lessons of growth and triumph that I have learned from Rolling's compelling story with those who need a reminder that they deserve a space to shine on the center stage of life! This is one of those books that transcends generational and demographic differences. Rolling's generosity and artistry will overwhelm you with gratitude and compel you to share it with others."

—**Dr. Sonny Kelly** - Author of *The Talk*

growing up

MEMOIRS OF A BLACK BOY DAYDREAMING

James Haywood Rolling, Jr.

SIMPLE WORD
PUBLICATIONS

Copyright © 2020 James Haywood Rolling, Jr.

All rights reserved. No part of this book may be reproduced, distributed, or transmitted in any form or by any means, including photocopying, recording, or other electronic or mechanical methods, without the prior written permission of the publisher, except in the case of brief quotations embodied in critical reviews and certain other noncommercial uses permitted by copyright law. For permission requests or related queries, please contact Simple Word Publications at inquiry@simplewordpublications.com.

Names: Rolling, James Haywood, 1963- author.
Title: Growing up ugly : memoirs of a black boy daydreaming / James Haywood Rolling, Jr.
Description: Fayetteville, NY : Simple Word Publications, 2020.
Identifiers: LCCN 2018906698 (print) | ISBN 978-1-937598-00-6 (paperback) | ISBN 978-1-937598-01-3 (ebook)
Subjects: LCSH: African Americans--Biography. | Artists--Biography. | Fathers and sons--Biography. | Blacks--Segregation--United States. | Psychological child abuse. | Autobiography. | BISAC: BIOGRAPHY & AUTOBIOGRAPHY / Cultural, Ethnic & Regional / African American & Black. | BIOGRAPHY & AUTOBIOGRAPHY / Artists, Architects, Photographers. | BIOGRAPHY & AUTOBIOGRAPHY / Personal Memoirs. | SELF-HELP / Personal Growth / Self-Esteem.
Classification: LCC E185.97.R65 A3 2020 (print) | LCC E185.97.R65 (ebook) | DDC 973.049/6073--dc23.

Front cover image by James Haywood Rolling, Jr.
Book design by Glen M. Edelstein, Hudson Valley Book Design

This memoir is a truthful recollection of actual events in the author's life. Some conversations have been recreated and/or supplemented. The names or details of some individuals and their stories have been changed or masked to respect their privacy.

This book is dedicated to anyone searching
for their creative superpower.

contents

preface

A CONVERSATION I HAD over a decade ago during a summer church ministry outreach triggered the writing of this little book. Sponsored by the Family Worship Center (FWC), our former church located in Clay, a suburb of Syracuse in Central New York, the outreach itself was offered deep in inner-city Syracuse to youngsters enrolled in a kind of mini-Vacation Bible School. As a trained artist, I had volunteered to do individual color pencil portraits of the young people we had gathered together on rows of folding chairs in a small outdoor lot in the heart of the urban community. My wife and I were new members of FWC at the time, and had only been attending worship services regularly for a few months prior to that summer youth program. FWC's founder, Reverend James Farley, had recently learned of my unique story of stumbling into a faith relationship with God while I was a youngster growing up in a rough Brooklyn neighborhood very similar to the Syracuse inner-city. As a boy, I'd suffered numerous verbal and physical abuses at home, on my block, and at school. I was rescued right on time and didn't even know it. Reverend Farley suggested that kids who had endured injuries similar to those I experienced might have much to gain from knowing the details of how I found healing and fulfillment in my own, transformed life. He encouraged me to share my story of surviving and, ultimately, thriving.

It has taken me far too many years to tell the whole story, but I've finally found the words. I offer them as a gift. If this book from *Simple Word Publications* speaks to you, please share it with the young people in your life. But even more importantly, cultivate and share your own story of how anyone can rise to a life worth giving.

For me, learning to give the best of myself to others began at the time in my life when God first met me at the point of my own greatest need. Whatever I have to share going forward is an everyday byproduct of the provisions I have learned to continually seek and receive from God whenever I find myself empty again.

acknowledgments

AFTER LANGUISHING FOR TOO long, this book was nursed back to health at a crucial stage by one of the most naturally giving people I am blessed to know. Thanks to Jacqueline Oliver for nudging me to tell the fuller story hidden beneath the surface, and for volunteering to be a line editor when I needed an urgent kickstart.

Thanks also to all my friends, colleagues, and fellow creatives who provided inspiration along the way.

Finally, thanks to my wife, Me'Shae, for her unwavering support no matter how many hours I put into this enterprise.

1
my ugliness

A moment of joy captured
when I was still able
to smile freely.

I USED TO THINK I was born ugly. I wasn't sure why in
the beginning. I couldn't pin down the source of my ill-fit-
tedness and out-of-placeness until I finally stared myself down
in a mirror one afternoon after being ridiculed by a little girl
whose name I don't remember. My ugliness wasn't some self-
harming assumption or the result of anyone else's intentional
misleading. Nor was it just because I had been born butt-first
rather than head-first—otherwise known as being a breech
baby. My ugliness was the built-up scar tissue of a childhood
spent tending to injuries I'd accumulated through a series of

unexpected pitfalls and penalties. The injury that lingered the longest was the revelation that my face was broken.

On sunny afternoons after school, kids from nearby surrounding blocks in Brooklyn came to our block to play because of its large, fenced-in schoolyard. Even with the absence of child-friendly playground equipment, games would break out across the schoolyard and spill out onto the sidewalks in front of several of the houses on Lincoln Place. Echoes cracked back and forth between the large apartment buildings and small red-orange brick houses on both sides of our narrow street, crowding the air with the pings of pounding rubber balls, scuffling shoe heels, sneakers slapping on asphalt, and the shouts of other children.

Sometimes white chalk would appear and hopscotch boxes were quickly drawn on the neat squares of pavement in front of my Grandma's house. Grandma lived right next door to us. On this particular day, I remember watching as a small flat stone was tossed to bounce across the cement into a numbered box. I watched the one-foot, two-feet, one-foot hops from box to box to stop and balance on one small hopping foot, each player finding their balance to drop a hand to pick up the stone. One little girl exited the parade to come sit beside me. I wasn't paying her any mind. She asked me to look at her. We were sitting on one of Grandma's two wooden benches, placed just inside the front gate opposite one another. Two steps down were the sidewalk and a bunch of other kids, still hopping. I didn't respond. I wasn't chatty. Instead, I turned my body away and avoided eye contact. Why was she talking to me anyway? Didn't she see I didn't have anything I wanted to say?

"Look at me! " she said, tugging at my arm.

"Will you stop it!" I snapped back at her, jerking my

arm away. Why was she bothering me? My eyebrows pulled toward the bridge of my nose into a frown.

"Smile!" the little girl said slyly, smiling herself, trying to lure me into disarmament.

"Leave me alone!" I yelled. I tried to slide down the bench, away from the manipulation. I must have grinned at that point. Maybe I was embarrassed by the attention, a personality trait that I continue to possess. Whatever my facial response was, the girl suddenly clapped a hand over her mouth, all giggles. I asked what she was laughing for. The kids playing hopscotch in front of us now had our attention as well. I can't remember the surrounding faces, just the noise and voices that seemed to stop. Making a show for her unexpected audience, the little girl stood up, pointed at me and declared, finger in my face, "Look! He only has _one_ dimple! See?! Look at his face!"

"No I don't," I said, dropping my eyes and my voice at the same time. Staring at the ground, I didn't want to look up to see if anyone was looking. My face warm and I needed to move away fast.

"No I don't," I repeated, stiffly. My whole head seemed to be on fire now. I was beneath windows on both sides of the street—some near, some far—a random clutter of onlookers. I rushed through the painted iron gate, painted just enough to hide the unstripped layers of paint beneath it, going quickly next door, up the stoop, into the vestibule, and then up the staircase covered with old linoleum to enter the second floor railroad-style apartment my family lived in. I stepped quietly through the slender hallway—so dark after the bright outside—around a curve and then left into the bathroom.

I locked the door with its frosted glass window. I didn't have to turn on the bathroom light to see. I just waited until sight came. There was a narrow light well in the center of the house, right beside the bathroom. My eyes adjusted to the dim sunlight working its way through the small window above and to the right of the toilet. It took a few seconds for my eyes to make out glowing particles of dust wafting upwards in gentle swirls through the light well's shaft. But at that moment, all I wanted was the dimness. I wanted the hard surfaces and inaccessibility. The silence in the bathroom welcomed me. The patterned tiled surfaces were a barricade, a force field of protection around my own bedeviled head space, keeping away the voices still curling toward my ears, still outside at play.

I climbed up to sit on the edge of the sink. It was clean, cold white porcelain. I had shorts on but the surface warmed quickly against my bare legs after the first biting contact. Carefully situating myself at dead center in front of the bathroom medicine cabinet mirror above the sink, I stared long at my face. The house was quiet. No one else was inside on such a beautiful day.

Everyone knew that you either have two dimples or no dimples at all. You could see that from all the illustrations and photographs of faces in books and magazines. You could see it on TV. I knew what normal people looked like. I could see well enough. And I'd seen enough to be certain. In the soft, chubby skin of my left cheek was the only dimple I could manage. Although I strained and poked at my tiring facial muscles, the flesh of my right cheek remained undented. I pushed with my tongue. I twisted my smile. I made my face move every way I could think of. I stared at my flaw. I figured out what I had to do next.

That was when I decided I would never let anyone else notice there was something wrong with me. I would never let anyone else see me smile. I couldn't fix ugly, but I could remove it from view.

Growing up, I was a hungry reader. Stories fed my superpower. Words on the printed page flexed to become agile muscles in my head. The stories I watched on television and in movie theaters would replay themselves in my imagination again and again, long after I turned the lights off and went to bed. Yet as a young boy in the late 1960s and early 1970s, I struggled to make sense of why there were so few faces like mine on TV, in movies, or illustrated in any of the books or comics I made short work of. I could see no brown-skinned little boys at all with my facial features and hair texture living outside of neighborhoods like the one I called home.

Starting in first grade, I was bused to a school several neighborhoods and gradations of skin color away from me in Sheepshead Bay—an overwhelmingly white neighborhood about an hour away, near Brighton Beach and Coney Island. My elementary school was a bright, clean building where I rarely encountered any other boy with lips as big as I imagined mine to be. I was one of a handful of African American kids at school, none of whom lived in that neighborhood. I did not want to stand out any more than I already did. I already knew I didn't fit in. If I smiled, my lips just stretched wider, drawing more attention to my having been born with a missing normality.

First to hide my condition—and, eventually, just to hide—I stopped smiling in the sight of others for over a decade throughout my childhood, only becoming comfortable doing so in public again well after I had exited my later teens. During those laughless years, I refused to be a child in front of strangers, friends, or family alike, so that I'd suffer no further embarrassment for not being born right. In the company of others, my primary effort was always to maintain my privacy and remain on the periphery of anyone else's attention. I strained not to giggle at a joke, or even crack a smile when someone tried to tickle me. It took great effort to maintain an unreadable façade from day to day, but these were acts of self-preservation. I did not *want* to be read. My ugliness was *my* business, no one else's. Like a box turtle, I made myself feel safe by hiding, abruptly vacuuming all the world could see of me back into the safety of my shell. Book closed. Sometimes when I wanted to be invisible, I slid into one of the handful of tiny closets in our small apartment—creating a self-fashioned sensory deprivation shelter for myself where anyone calling my name remained easy to ignore, muffled by hanging clothes pressed against each of my ears. The outlines of my slender contours were pleasantly erased even to my own eyes by the darkness and indiscernible clutter. Sometimes I simply buried the whole of my body in the uppermost bunk bed in the cramped bedroom I shared with my brothers when we were younger. I would wedge myself against the wall, folded over by the protective ceiling, shielded under the warm covers, daydreaming.

Years later, long after I'd finally accepted that a one-dimpled face wasn't actually a deformity—and well into my premature and *why-so-serious* young adulthood—I still couldn't shake the learned reflex to retract into the multi-level maze of my Snoopy's doghouse imagination, cocooned from any undesired contact or connection. I had disciplined myself to pull back in a snap so I could defend all the parts of me that were vulnerable to injury. Yet, I was also tearing my own flesh in the fastening mechanism over and over and over again—almost as often as my painful habit of accidently crunching the insides of my baby fatted cheeks while chewing my food. Either way, I could taste the blood in my mouth.

Caged Bird

And if you must sing
sing softly
or they will hear you
and rush to cover your cage
with a form-fitting sheath
smothering the frame
that once captured the sun on its wire rails
along with all the life within it

2

crown heights

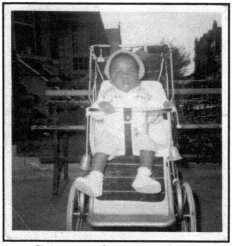

Sitting out on the stoop next door at
Grandma and Grandpa's house.

WHEN I WAS A BOY I lived in a ghetto in central Brooklyn, one of the five great boroughs of New York City. People might think a neighborhood with a fancy name like Crown Heights couldn't possibly be a ghetto. Some folks might even argue that *their* section of Crown Heights was not a ghetto at all. But the block on Lincoln Place between Troy and Schenectady Avenues, where I grew up, was definitely a ghetto. You know you live in a ghetto when from time to time—and to no one's surprise—a few of the neighborhood boys would sneak up to the rooftops of the tallest apartment buildings on the corner to shoot off their guns into the night sky just for fun.

Actually, our block was more like a neighborhood within a neighborhood. Our stretch of Lincoln Place had so many charming little two-family homes with their own backyards or driveways that any average New Yorker could tell that our street was once a most pleasant place to call home. Yet, when I was a child growing up on our street, I ran from gangs like the Jolly Stompers—none of whose phantom members I ever personally saw by the way, since I would scatter in make-believe fright like all the other kids at the mere mention that they were coming our way. Maybe it was just a silly game, a conjured-up reason to run and scream. Maybe they were never really coming. But I'm willing to bet that there were very few other neighborhoods in Brooklyn where child's play involved pretending to run away from a violent street gang.

In my part of Brooklyn, the one tree that grew in our backyard was there only because it had pushed its way past a corner of cement and no one had bothered to uproot it before it was too late. We attached a clothesline to this tree from the kitchen window of our second-floor apartment, but that's about all we could do with it. It was one of those weed trees that grew in Brooklyn, the *Ailanthus Altissima*, neither a great oak or maple like those in some of the whiter neighborhoods, but an intrepid invader that had found a seam of inhospitable earth and bullied in its roots. An *Ailanthus Altissima* is equipped to survive a city's filth, shoot up fast, stink the air, and die young. Its branches were too weak for treehouses or tire swings. Looking out from our window, one could view the impropriety of this near useless tree, framed by an over-large apartment building that blocked out the sky from across the debris-filled back alleyway between the Rolling family property and the other half of the block facing a parallel boulevard, the always busy Eastern Parkway. If I looked long enough, the rear-facing wall of the apartment building directly across from us sometimes revealed portraits that were as still as I was, each one looking back at me through windows punched in brick. At other times all that was visible were fleeting cinematic shadows through torn eggshell-colored roller shades or faded bed sheets hung in windows for an imperfect privacy.

My parents told me that just before I was born there was a "white flight" from Crown Heights, which had historically been a high-class residential neighborhood where wealthy Manhattanites maintained second homes. Their "flight" meant that many of the former residents of Crown Heights and other nearby Brooklyn neighborhoods like East New York and Brownsville had packed up and fled our block for the eastern suburbs of Long Island as, one by one, homeowners with darker skin began pouring in with their families in tow. In 1960, Crown Heights was 70 percent white and approximately 50 to 60 percent Jewish; by 1970, it was 70 percent comprised of Blacks who had moved up from the South, with a large number of immigrants from the Caribbean. At the time I was growing up there, the clear majority of the folks in my area of Crown Heights had African American, West Indian, and Puerto Rican origins. The only significant number of whites left in our area consisted of a fairly large community of ultra-Orthodox Jews, distinguished by the all-black clothing and ankle-length coats worn by men, the wide-brimmed black hats that even little boys wore, and caravans of baby carriages pushed by women in plain, unattractive dresses. The Chabad-Lubavitch religious sect had carved out and bought up whole blocks of residential and commercial real estate along Eastern Parkway which were just a few streets down from large communities of color, yet always felt worlds away.

At the corner of Schenectady Avenue and Lincoln Place stood Public School 167. It was a towering brick and stone structure with parapets that gave it the look of a great castle, like the ones in books and movies. The painted white parapets of P.S. 167 were remnants left behind in the flight of those whites that fled Crown Heights when the demographics began to darken, except for a few like Dr. Schwartz, my mother's family doctor ever since she was a little girl. Located on Kosciusko Street in the adjacent neighborhood of Bedford-Stuyvesant, Dr. Schwartz was the family doctor of all my mother's young children. I have unwanted memories of my pants being pulled down in front of my mother, with Dr. Schwartz's big gray-haired ungloved hand placed rudely on my bare scrotum, checking the old-fashioned way for any swelling that might signal the mumps at each increasingly infrequent visit. Dr. Schwartz stayed and practiced medicine in the changing neighborhood until he died. As Crown Heights was abandoned by wealthier, white Protestant families, it was also drained of its tax base, rapidly deteriorating into a ghetto. The school building on my corner also succumbed to the neglect common to large U.S. urban cities during that era, in spite of its impressive façade. If you looked close enough, you could see the white paint on the parapets of P.S. 167 was weather-beaten and chipped.

*　　*　　*

P.S. 167 was the elementary school zoned to serve our neighborhood's residents—a school I never personally attended, situated alongside a large, cement-top schoolyard that had no grass or trees. Chain-link fences as high as some nearby rooftops extended from the school walls to complete the enclosure of the sprawling courtyard used for recess, morning line-up, and dismissal. But the school's recess area was also the neighborhood's only playground for blocks around, unless you were old enough to safely navigate a game of stickball in the street while dodging cars as they periodically drove down the block. P.S. 167's tall schoolyard fences were punctuated with several basketball courts, battered backboards, bent hoops, and the shredded remnants of basketball nets, each spaced at even intervals along the fencing's support posts. Even after the large street-side entrance gates into P.S. 167 schoolyard were padlocked at the end of the school day, the courts still filled up with kids who had dashed nimbly over the fence tops or scrambled through one of several conveniently placed rips in the fabric of chain links.

The massive, jutting exterior walls and arched entranceways to the school formed the other two sides of the yard's perimeter. Along certain portions of the wall, which was painted deep red, there was a seemingly unbroken scrawl of curse words, gang tags, and "Tyrone was here" graffiti. As if nursing a bad rash that kept on resurfacing, the building's custodians covered the near-daily vandalism with bandages of paint again and again, never quite able to match the newest patch of red to the previous layer.

After dark, some of the boys on our block could find nothing better to do than to rebel against the silence expected with the coming of night. They collected empty or half-filled beer and soda bottles that had been carelessly discarded— left to litter the street gutter, the short stone walls, or the small sets of stairs around the perimeter of the schoolyard. And then, one by one, they busted each container against random walls or gray slate steps, launching small slow-motion explosions of a million grains of sparkling dust. Every detonation of exploding glass rocketed off the surfaces of the school's property and then echoed up and down the canyon of buildings along Lincoln Place. The job of carefully cleaning up all the larger shards of broken glass in the days that followed these destructive nights fell not only to the school's custodians, but also to grown-ups and kids like me from around the neighborhood who played handball or paddleball after school and on weekends against sections of the schoolyard walls where we'd painted the lines of the ball courts ourselves.

Rear Window

Once every 20 years or so
I am reminded of where I began

Looking out from the kitchen of our second-floor apartment
a vista of apartment buildings dominates our view
across the chasm
between the Rolling property
and the rest of Crown Heights

I dared not cross

On the other side
across the fence just beyond the cracks
in our house's concrete-covered backyard
through windows punched in cinderblock and brick
there were living still-life portraits
fleeting cinematic shadows
never leaving their frames
guarding all hope and resilient grit
as faces peeked through rips
in drawn eggshell shades
and faded bedsheets
draped for semi-privacy
like haphazard patches
within the dense fenestration

There shouldn't be prisons
in Brooklyn where I lived,
but there are apartment buildings

They persist and recur in my memory
in spite of progressive social policy

3

sketches from 1260

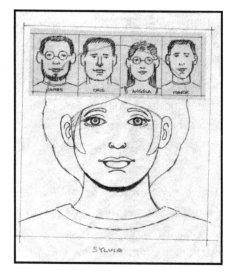

Sketches of the Rolling family made by my
father for a book he never completed.

I WAS THE OLDEST of the four kids in my family—three
boys and a girl. Several years ago, I happened across drawings
my father had sketched for an unpublished illustrated memoir
laying at the bottom of a flat file drawer in his curtained and
quieted art studio. On browning layers of superimposed
tracing paper, edges torn and brittle, my mother, Sylvia, is
recreated as a black fine point marker schematic; de-aged, it
is my mother in the beauty of her youth. Above her head float

her four children in order of birth, James Haywood, Dwayne Christopher (who everyone just called Chris), Angela Evette, and Mark Edward. Apparently intended to be page 1 of the illustrated memoir he had authored, this initial discovery was followed by 40 pages on cheap copy paper, alternating between text and full-page image blocks. Within the image blocks are 20 absences, images unrecorded. Jim Rolling begins with his mother, who coincidentally shared the same first name as his grandmother on his father's side and was therefore distinguished as "Little Eva." My great-grandmother Eva, whom my father called Gram, outlived my grandmother Eva by nearly twenty years. A small scrap of handwritten notes, perhaps intended to accompany the first drawing in my father's unfinished picture book, is attached to the second page by a bit of transparent tape. My father wrote:

> Little Eva, my mother, one of the first women to drive a trolley. Sometimes I would meet her as she drove past our building on Rockaway Avenue. "Here' your lunch Gram made for you," I would say as I handed her a brown paper bag. She was twice a heroine. Had write-ups in the *Amsterdam News*. Black Woman Driver Saves Passengers When Trolley Catches On Fire.

Our parents raised Chris, Angie, Mark, and I in a railroad-thin apartment on the second floor of a walk-up building at 1260 Lincoln Place, part of a string of attached row houses along our narrow street in Brooklyn. The house was defiantly purchased by my father's grandmother even though it was smack in the middle of the pre-white flight Crown Heights after she'd won about $40,000 playing "the numbers"—an illegal form of gambling nevertheless prevalent among disenfranchised African Americans in the early 20th century, equivalent in many ways to our modern state lottery system. $40,000 was a HUGE amount of money at the time. Whenever any of us told friends we were hanging out with that we "had to go back to our house," we were really just talking about our second-floor apartment in Gram's house. In fact, when I was very little, Gram still lived downstairs with her son Elmo, my father's uncle. Uncle Elmo, who used to drive a cab for a living, had one eye. Uncle Elmo was as tall and silent and drained of color as Lurch, the giant butler in the old black and white *Addams Family* television reruns I used to love watching. Actually, I don't remember Uncle Elmo ever having much to say to me at all. He'd walk right by me if I didn't greet him first, in deference to him as my elder.

* * *

My mother once saved my life, as children's mothers often do. I was no more than 5 or 6 years old. I remember being brought one day to the children's clinic at Kings County Hospital Center. I was walking alone behind Ma, balancing along the yellow painted cement curb of the traffic circle leading up to the main entrance for drop-off and pick-up of patients, with both my arms sticking straight out like one long steadying beam. My mother told me to be careful but I was feeling a bit adventurous and I'd always had quick reflexes and sure footing. Nevertheless, I remember losing my balance and landing with a surprised thud in the street lined with bumper to bumper idling vehicles. I had landed beneath a yellow taxi cab. I remember turning my head and staring at the tread of a car tire, up close so that I could see all of its black zig-zaggy surface details from a point of view that was entirely new to me. That's when, almost immediately, the tire started to roll toward my face. It was stop-and-start traffic and the tire's movement was at first almost imperceptible in that second before it would crush my skull. Of course, I didn't know how to react. I'd never been in a life-threatening position before. In fact, I didn't have *time* to react since I was already face to face with the moving tire. I didn't think to cry out in fear or alarm as it has never been my nature to startle easily or cry out for help. Apparently, my height and slight frame prevented the driver from noticing either my approach or my sudden disappearance, so he had no clue that a child had fallen under his vehicle's wheels. That's when, with a shout of "Jim-Jim!!," I felt a sudden yank on my jacketed arm and I was face to face with Ma, her voice simultaneously expressing as much anger as it signaled her relief.

* * *

The next time I had a near-death experience, nobody was there to pluck me to safety. I was bicycling down a notoriously steep hill, many blocks long, leading away from Crown Heights down to an adjacent neighborhood. Full of adolescent adventure and invincibility, I allowed my bike to pick up speed without applying the brakes periodically along the way. I realized this was a mistake at the same time I also realized my brakes were too worn to effectively slow my descent at the speed I was now coming down the hill. I was on a wide street with lots of traffic, heading fast toward a busy intersection. The problem I faced was the recognition I would arrive at the cross street just as the light turned red and that there was no way I'd be able to safely stop. For some reason, I didn't panic.

Instead I calculated my best odds in the split seconds just before I arrived at the red light. In order not to be struck by oncoming traffic, I would have to turn left at the intersection into the direction of the cross-traffic that now had the green light. As I hit the intersection, cars were already beginning to pull out in front of me and the only way I could make the turn at the speed I was travelling was to make as wide a turn as possible. Otherwise I could sense I was going to pitch over and land underneath the tires of several approaching vehicles—which was definitely not the conclusion to the bike ride I had planned on when I left the house! Still invincible apparently, I surprised myself when my planned maneuver actually worked. Almost.

I was now headed 90 degrees to the left of my previous direction, but my speed was not diminished. Rather, I found myself zooming along in the same direction and pace as vehicles that were just moments before starting to cross in front of me—vehicles now picking up speed. I had ended up sidelong against one of them, slightly off balance, my hand leaning atop the car's hood trying to correct my dangerous tilt. Steering my 10-speed bike only with my weaker left hand, I gave a slight push off the automobile with my right hand to regain my balance and that's when it happened. My handlebars jerked inward towards the traveling vehicle I was keeping pace with, and my front wheel immediately jammed to the right as well. Over the handlebars I flew. First, I saw asphalt. Then I saw the spinning front tire of the car next to my face. I saw blue sky. I heard a woman scream from across the street. Time slowed down as I somersaulted through points of view I had never before experienced. I saw the blacktop asphalt again. I saw the spinning rear tire of the car next to my face. I saw blue sky. Then I looked down and saw I was standing on both my feet. I looked behind me, half expecting to see another car bearing down on where I stood, but there happened to be a huge gap in the traffic at that point. The street was clear enough for me to hustle out of harm's way. I looked in front of me and the car that had unexpectedly become my travelling companion was pulled to the side as the driver ran back to check on my condition. I shuffled to collect my twisted bicycle laying in the middle of the road. Folks ran up to me to ask if I was okay and warned me that I might have struck my head and to stand there a moment. Fortunately, I hadn't. All I had was some road rash and bleeding on my bare arm and the side of my knee beneath my pants. I limped home, walking beside my bike back up the hill toward 1260 Lincoln Place. I was fortunate. I was blessed. My life was not intended to end that day.

*   *   *

As the oldest child, I was often sent on shopping errands. I either went down to the corner of Lincoln Place and Schenectady Avenue to what we called the "Spanish store" (owned by a Puerto Rican family); or to the Key Food supermarket on Schenectady (which *always* smelled like fresh rat bait); or to the A&P supermarket on St. John's Place just around the corner (where the prices were way too high). Honestly, around the corner always felt so much like another neighborhood to me that I hardly went to the A&P anyway. If I needed to pick up vegetables or fruits, I went to the "Korean store" on Schenectady, near the hustle and bustle of Eastern Parkway.

Sometimes leaving the block where I grew up just felt dangerous. The east end corner of Lincoln Place intersected with Schenectady Avenue. At that intersection, you turned past the schoolyard walked one short block and was confronted with six lanes of traffic along Eastern Parkway, with its apartment buildings, shops, and the always busy Utica Avenue station of the IRT subway line—the first stop and a major connecting hub on the way to Manhattan. The west end corner of my block intersected Troy Avenue, with its clutter of overcrowded apartment buildings, shadowy doorways, sketchy characters, and sidewalks that stank of fermented urine, all of which were misplaced on a block with as many quiet, residential homes as ours had. That corner of Troy and Lincoln Place was notorious for its 24/7 drug dealing, nighttime gunshots, and all manner of incidents folks only spoke about in whispers. People got arrested at the corner of Lincoln Place and Troy. One handsome, popular kid named Kevin got shot in the head and died on that corner. As a kid, I used to see him on the block almost every day and then I never saw him again, as if his page had just been ripped out of a book I should know every word of, leaving it all up to me not to forget his face or his name.

My maternal grandmother happened to live right next door to us at 1258 Lincoln Place along with her two sons, Ma's older brothers Uncle Sonny and Uncle Eddie. There must have been lots of nice houses for sale all at once during those 10 years when the whites in Crown Heights flew away. For a good while, Grandma's oldest daughter, my Aunt Muriel, lived right across the street with her kids, too. In fact, it seemed like most of my many first cousins could be found right on Lincoln Place on any given day. Grandma used to cook dishes that smelled delicious but I could never convince myself to eat her fish-head soup and dumplings, a traditional Caribbean meal from her home country of Nevis, the sister island of St. Kitts in the British West Indies. Well, I'd eat the dumplings at the most. I was told that when they were young, Grandma met Grandpa on a boat headed to the United States. For years, that's what I always told people about my mother's side of the family tree, but there's more to the story.

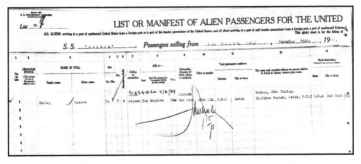

Documentation of Grandma's immigration to the United States
nearly 100 years ago.

I recently discovered the original ship's manifest listing the transport and date of the immigration of my mother's mother, Miriam Susan Alberta Hanley, sailing out aboard the S.S. Guiana and departing from the island of St. Kitts in the British West Indies on Dec. 20, 1923 to arrive safely as an alien passenger to the United States on Dec. 27, 1923. Here are some facts according to this document. Grandma was 20 years old when she arrived in the United States and her occupation was listed as a "Seamstress." In its upper left-hand corner, this particular document bears the imprint of the U.S. Department of Labor, which kept track of such things. This document also identifies Grandma as a native of the parish of St. John's on the island of Nevis, and the daughter of John Hanley, one of my great-grandfathers on my mother's side. Finally, it lists Grandma's destination as New York City where she would soon fall in love with young Mr. Lawrence, who also immigrated from Nevis. However, I also discovered the original ship's manifest listing the transport and date of the immigration of my mother's father—evidence that my grandmother and grandfather did NOT arrive on the same boat at all.

Documentation of Grandpa's immigration to the United States, four months before Grandma.

In the eighth row of the original ship's manifest listing the transport and date of the immigration of my mother's father, Edward Darrell Lawrence, it shows that Grandpa arrived in the United States aboard the S.S. Parima on Aug. 26, 1923 at the age of 18 years old, having departed from the island of St. Kitts a week earlier on Aug. 18, 1923 just four months before Grandma. His occupation at the time was listed as a "Domestic" worker. Grandpa is also listed as the son of J. Lawrence, my other great-grandfather on my mother's side, originating from the parish of St. Thomas one of the five parishes that comprise the island of Nevis. My mother, whose maiden name was Sylvia Juanita Lawrence, is the youngest and only surviving sibling of the four children produced from Grandma and Grandpa's union. We were just blessed to be able to celebrate Ma's 80th birthday last year.

Family photographs of Grandpa and Grandma, my mother's parents.

Grandma had asthma like I did, though a much worse form of it. As a boy, I liked sitting in her bedroom and listening to Family Radio, a national network of conservative Christian programming broadcast locally in Brooklyn on the WFME station. Grandma's accent sounded like organ music to me. I never talked much as I sat with her in the stillness of her bright, bay-windowed bedroom. The quiet made me happy as hymns from the radio and the melodies of her voice collided and cascaded together with shafts of light down the room's sun-washed walls, settling into my ears, settling into my spirit. Plus, because she was one of the few family members at 1258 Lincoln Place who did not smoke, I could breathe freely in her bedroom. In that intersection of sensations, I knew I was loved. I don't remember my Grandpa as well. Grandpa died in 1965 when I was very young. One remaining memory is this: If I was misbehaving as a toddler, he'd break off a switch from the hedges in front of our house, strip the small leaves from the thin branch, and give me a quick, gentle swat or two on my legs. I really wish I had grown up with Grandpa in my life a little longer.

Fall Rising

Greetings—
season of my childhood;

The steady wash of passing rain
layers city in shadow and gray
lowering veils of somnolent sound
over my searching eyes;
through the dripping pane
I see doorways fill
with outlined faces stranded in the storm;
trees are shorn of drying leaves;
water rhythms play my rooftop;
left am I in a daydream...

Taken in the arms of Melancholy
I know that I am loved;
remembrances of safe isolation
of sitting still by my bedroom window
observing the other world living out there
absolutely removed from my window chair;

Circle my mind in this empty square

As through the fog of my breath on cold glass
I rub with the palm of my hand
and open a tunnel;
I watch the street become a stream
car wheels slashing through its flow
currents rising along blacktop gutters
sweeping paper, empty cans, and dead leaves

down around beneath parked cars
to clog at the corner storm sewers...

The return of Autumn begins with cold rain
and the spine-tingling chill I so enjoy
such that goose bumps rise and body shivers
and I smile like a child
at my old best friend
who's come to visit me one more year.

4

father figure

Self-portrait by Jim Rolling, for the cover of
a magazine in which he was featured.

I WAS NAMED AFTER my father, just as he was named after
his. My father nevertheless insisted on being called Jim instead of
James, his given name. As a consequence of his name preference,
and as my father's first son, around my block I was known as
Jim-Jim. I never liked this nickname but it stuck. To this day, even

though much of my hair is either gone or gone gray, anyone who lived on Lincoln Place during my childhood still calls me Jim-Jim.

My father was born and raised as an only child in the Brownsville neighborhood of Brooklyn. At one point, his family also lived in the Bowery, a ramshackle neighborhood in the southern portion of Manhattan just north of Chinatown known during much of the 20th century as New York City's "Skid Row." Eventually his family moved to Bedford-Stuyvesant, also in Brooklyn, before eventually settling at 1260 Lincoln Place in the bordering neighborhood of Crown Heights. My father's father, James Rolling, was the son of Lynn Van Buren Rolling and Eva E. Haywood, who were married in 1913 and originally started their family in Mustang, Oklahoma before their relocation to New York City. I have no family photographs of my paternal grandfather.

Death certificate of my grandfather, James Rolling.

According to his death certificate, James Rolling was a general loading dock worker when he died of "chronic pulmonary tuberculosis" at around 6:00 AM on January 17, 1939 at Sea View Hospital in the borough of Staten Island at the tragic age of 21. My own father was only about a year old at the time. Because of unequal access to health care at the time of my grandfather's death in 1939—well before the discovery of the successful antibiotic streptomycin in 1943— the rate at which tuberculosis prematurely consumed the lives of African Americans whose lungs were infected with the bacteria was usually two to three times the mortality rate of whites in the United States. In particular, an attending physician noted that my grandfather's lungs showed evidence of hydropneumothorax having contributed to his death, with so much damage that there was fluid found at the bottom of both lungs with air circulating only on the top. James Rolling was buried at Evergreen Cemetery, which borders both Brooklyn and Queens, but the greater calamity of the Rolling family lineage is that his older sister had been buried in that very same cemetery just five years earlier.

My paternal grandfather was the youngest of three children born from the union of my great-grandparents. It turns out that the oldest sibling born of that union, Louise Rolling, *also* succumbed to pulmonary tuberculosis at the heart-breaking age of 20 years, 3 months, and 26 days old on the date of Oct. 27, 1934, five years before my grand-father died of the same awful disease. In the end, two thirds of my great-grandparent's offspring were killed off by tuber-culosis before they ever had an opportunity to fully enter their adulthood. It's no wonder the surviving middle child, my father's Uncle Elmo, never had much to say. Having lost both his big sister and his little brother to the same disease

within the space of five years, Uncle Elmo had apparently
lived a traumatized life. Uncle Elmo lived downstairs in our
house at 1260 Lincoln Place until he finally died in 1979.
His mother Eva (whom we affectionately called "Gram") also
lived at 1260 Lincoln Place until she died in 1983, outliving
all of her children.

Death certificate of my grandfather's big sister,
Louise Rolling, who also died of tuberculosis.

Gram had a few brothers, but one of my father's grand-
uncles figured prominently in his lifelong aversion to
attending church. One of Gram's older brothers was a key
figure in the pastoral lineage of the St. Paul Community Baptist

Church which was established in 1927 when 15 worshippers formed a fellowship at 265 Thatford Avenue, a storefront in the Brownsville section of Brooklyn. Initially called the St. Paul Community Mission when it was officially organized, one of the original members of that congregation was Edward Leonard Haywood, who assumed the role of the Mission's leader. He would eventually be installed as its second pastor, serving in that capacity from 1929-1935, and continued to have a leadership role in the congregation when he was succeeded by its next pastor. On one of the unfinished pages of my father's unpublished illustrated memoir, he notes that although his granduncle Ed was a prominent minister in Brownsville's biggest church at the time, he also took advantage of his family and friends in ways that left a permanent mark. My father told me more than once that there was a period in his childhood where he was required to attend St. Paul's, located in walking distance of where the Rolling family also lived, not just on Sunday, but *every day*. It was all too much for my father.

At the time of his untimely death, my grandfather James was married to Eva B. Rolling, a woman who coincidentally had the same given name as his own mother. Originally named Eva Bly Hart, my paternal grandmother was a flamboyant and outspoken woman who was often involved in local theater productions. She died of lung cancer in 1965 at the age of 48 before I had turned 3 years old or we ever had an opportunity to bond. Because she was likely fighting off her illness since the time I was born, she did not have the extra energy to babysit me as most grandmothers do. I never even had a chance to develop an affectionate name for her since I was still learning to talk as she was dying. She was never Grandma or Gram—in my memory she remains veiled, and in this writing she's just my father's mother. She was cared for at home during the last stages of her life and, despite my only being a toddler, I do have a faint recollection of that period of time, filled with dimly lit rooms and lots of whispers behind thick, stale-smelling curtains I was not allowed to peek around.

Unlike most other men working as general laborers in my neighborhood—men who either drove a bus or taxi or were subway train conductors or track-workers or hauled garbage off the curb for the sanitation department—my father never had a blue-collar job. He was proud to boast that he'd been a working artist since he was 18 years old and joined the military. A veteran of the U.S. Army, my father was put to work as an Army illustrator, responsible for producing graphic designs that were used in Army publications, signs, charts, and posters. I found the following sketch one day in a sealed envelope in a flat file drawer kept in his studio. It startled me not only because I was an adult at the time of its discovery, but also because my father had never thought to share it with me as a child or as a young art student. I had become an accomplished portrait artist over the years, as indicated by the cover image I created for the book you are currently reading. My father was well aware of my love for drawing since I had completed several of my best portraits on an easel in his studio. I was proud of my skill. Yet here was evidence of warmly realized, carefully studied black and white pencil portraits of his Army buddies from a man who had never developed a habit of being warm to me. I had become very familiar with the many, many illustrations and creatures my father had created at his drafting table over the years as a graphic artist. *These* drawings were entirely new to me. I knew from experience how intimate the making of a live portrait is. Although these drawings were completed nearly two years before I was born, my father had invested real love into each skillful rendering. I could see it. I could immediately see his love and passion for accurately capturing the details of each face peeking through the soft-hewn marks. These brothers-in-arms who served with my father, although he was an only child, were brought to life in my hands as if they were his family members, and were breathing again in front of my eyes on carefully preserved pages of decades-old lined ledger paper. When I asked my father about these secret drawings, he said, "History is important." I had never heard those words from him before then.

Portrait of an Army buddy at Fort Dix, sketched by my father nearly 2 years before I was born.

Although my father presented himself as a rigidly disciplined man since most of his artistic skills were self-taught, in fact, he was not. His rigidity served only as camouflage for unspeakable behavior behind closed doors, only some of which is my story to tell. What I can say is that he was a white-collar professional, a commercial artist who started his career at J. C. Penney department stores, designing product displays and rising through the ranks from 1967 through 1977 to become Supervisor of Design and Display Lettering Manager, which included inventing original typefaces for the retailer's Display Department. Early on when my father was still only assigned to do posters at J. C. Penney, the creative director at that time started drawing upon the work of American abstract expressionist and minimalist painter, Frank Stella. Stella had developed what my father called "a nice tight style," featuring the use of brightly colored geometric patterns with simple intersecting circles and lines. My father once said that Stella's work had a huge influence on him professionally. When my father first started designing typefaces (where you once had to individually design every single letter from A-Z as a cohesive whole), he also became a great fan of the work of the renowned American typographer and lettering artist Ed Benguiat, a man he spoke of reverently as "the greatest type designer in the world."

After leaving J. C. Penney and spending the next two years as a freelance designer at Barry Waldman Studios from 1977 to 1979, my father went to work from 1979 to 1991 as an art director for the Newspaper Advertising Bureau, Inc., which represented 800 member newspapers. There he advanced to the level of Senior Designer, developing and launching national campaigns to promote newspaper business. Sometimes he painted portraits of family and friends for special occasions, but he lamented getting away from his early experiments and adventures as an artist.

My father's hand-drawn business card as his
freelance career first got rolling.

The following drawing, of a kitten at play, was sent to me out of the blue in December of 2016 by a woman named June whom I had never met before and resides in Florida. She was cleaning out the homes of both her grandmother and great-grandmother a few years ago and found a signed drawing preserved in a large aging envelope with the name "James H. Rolling" and the address "1260 Lincoln Pl." written in one corner. She looked up my email address on the internet and began a correspondence one night as to the

Pencil drawing of a kitten at play sketched by my father
sometime after high school.

source of this drawing. I told her I immediately recognized my
father's signature and that the mailing address was ours as well.
We then tried to determine if my father's drawing ended up in
the home of one of her immediate family members because we
were all somehow related. At the end of our initial exchange
that evening, June recognized some of the relationships I was
recounting and asked: "OK, connection – Eva Bly Rolling.
Does that name mean anything to you?" I told June excitedly
that it was the name of my father's mother and that she and
I must be cousins. It became apparent that this drawing was
created by my father as a lesson assignment response, most likely
in the *Famous Artists School* at-home self-study correspondence
course he once told me was his only option to continue his
study of art after high school, given his inability to afford the
time or expenses needed to enroll in college. This drawing was
just a continuation of the kind of self-study experiments my
father had committed himself to since he was in high school.
As flawed as he was, self-study was one of my father's creative
superpowers, all of which would be on display at 1260 Lincoln

Place for years after he painted an extensive mural connecting across the walls of the small first floor bathroom.

Years ago I did paintings on the walls down in the bathroom. I did some fish. I decided then to use oils. I was in high school at the time. But I wasn't doing oil paintings in high school—what I did on the wall (and I didn't finish it), was better than my school work because I was kind of doing something on my own. I took one of those *Life* annual manuals…magazines, books…and I picked some fish pages, pages with fish, and I kind of put together a concept of the fish swimming under the water, with a blue background, and then I painted the fish. That was like the first painting I did and I kind of went away from it because of job reasons, for family…I had to make a living. I don't have the luxury now, but I realize that there are things you should do, whether you have the luxury of doing them or not. Over the years you read about artists that kind of suffer and kind of have a single-mindedness of purpose and then years later the money comes. Money doesn't come right away. You kind of decide what you want to do and stick to it. My mother wrote an expression. She said, "Do what you have a flair for doing and if you're good enough at it, the money will come." That's something she wrote and I had a card that I used to keep on the mirror… because she used to say, "Don't worry about the money." [I mean] her and my relatives that loved and supported me, even though they couldn't see me making money as an artist. At that time, if you got a job working for transit you could retire [with a pension]…you didn't have to worry about paying the bills, and that was considered a good job. Being an artist was like…one of my uncles thought I was crazy because I wanted to be an artist, and he said, "You'll never make any money being an artist."

My father was proud of defying all those expectations and predictions. He let me use his supplies occasionally, and I first taught myself to draw and tell stories in his art studio. In hindsight, I imagine I might never have become an artist or an art teacher had I not grown up in the shadow of my father. Apart from these small acts of generosity with his arts supplies, my father didn't have much to do with me from day to day. And he didn't have much to say to me either unless he was scolding me or calling me a "birdbrain." It was made clear that my father was too busy to make time to include me in his world on a regular basis. He was private, quiet, secretive, and expressed no real curiosity in hearing what was on my mind. We did not have father-son chats about my school day or go fishing together or play basketball on the weekends. Every once in a while, he took us all bowling. I can still sometimes remember the smell of the burgers and fries he fed us there when I'm struck by a similar smell wafting through the air as I walk through the city. I think the bowling alley he preferred was near Empire Roller Skating Center at Empire Boulevard near Bedford Avenue, where for years folks of all ages went to skate and sweat all night and stay out of trouble, under a swirl of spinning lights and thumping sound. A couple of times each summer we'd all load into the car for a family picnic at a nearby state park. But something was always off-kilter between us. This recognition that our family dynamics were strained was evident on long car trips when almost imme-diately the radio would get switched on and dialed up loud to disguise the fact that we really didn't talk much with one another. My father always maintained a "children are better seen and not heard" approach to raising us, also evident in that we typically didn't eat meals together as a family—not breakfast, not lunch, and not dinner. Frankly, there was no room for a family of six around our kitchen table anyway, and the apartment was too small for any of its rooms to be used solely for us to gather to dine. So whenever food was prepared, out of necessity we each had a habit of floating through the kitchen like space satellites orbiting in and out of each other's vicinity.

I do remember my father bringing me to his office on rare occasions to see where he worked in Manhattan in one of the skyscrapers on the Avenue of the Americas. He was proud of his button-down shirt and tie job. I enjoyed seeing glimpses of the world beyond our little corner of Crown Heights. But what my father shared most freely were his punishing lectures where I was ordered to stand absolutely still and bite my tongue as he chided me with his usual line: "I know you better than you know yourself." If he really did believe he knew all he needed to know about who I was, perhaps that explains why he spent so little time building a relationship that felt safe or secure to me. As he loomed large over my life, physically cornering me against a wall at the top of the staircase more times than I'd like to remember, it seemed like he saw in me the parts of himself that he knew and hated.

As I became a more precocious youngster, I grew profoundly afraid of my father's presence. And fear is far from being the same thing as respect. Starting when I was still very small, I'd gotten used to the flash of his hard knuckles, out of the blue, slamming into my belly or upside my head. This happened when unknowingly, from time to time, I had offended his strict notion of common sense. I got accustomed to being suddenly doubled over in pain from a blow to the stomach, or being struck dizzy. While I was momentarily stunned, only then would he tell me what I had done "wrong."

Not being able to figure out my father's rules kept me off balance. One day, my father noticed that I'd developed some automatic responses—a duck of the head, a bob, a weave, a quick and cat-like twist of the body—whenever his hand appeared unexpectedly along the edges of my field of view. Because I've always had a very acute sense of peripheral vision, I began flinching out of reflex even if he just happened to be reaching for a cup from the dish rack over my shoulder. I remember my surprise, and relief, when he told me one day he'd become aware of my new habits and would try to stop striking me so often.

*   *   *

Nevertheless, over time it was obvious that my father preferred to generate a never-ending list of quibbles with me as well as my siblings. He made it a point to emphasize almost every day that we were not yet trustworthy in a number of ways, but especially in that we were not really allowed to bring our friends into "his" house without his prior approval. To be honest, his suspicion and accusations seemed to border on paranoia at times. While my father was still alive, he accused me of everything from growing a beard so as not to *look* like him, to choosing architecture as my high school concentration and my college major so as not to *be* like him.

My father did however teach me many things, both directly and indirectly. Hence, I quickly developed my *own* set of rules to live by. Good rules. Consistent rules. One evening in particular, I got offended at my mother for breaking one of my biggest rules. Now I freely admit that I was rigid. Rules were important to me. They were like the guide rails that kept me from tumbling out of the top bunk of our beds while I was sleeping. More than once as a child I was shocked to consciousness after a crash to the cold floor in the middle of the night—trust me, it was not pleasant picking myself afterwards! I figured out early on that I was safer knowing what the rules were. And once I knew the rules, you didn't have to tell me twice. For example, if I tossed something into a trash can and missed, I HAD to go back and pick it up and put it where it belonged. Telling the truth was another of my internal rules. Rules mattered. Rules kept me from dying.

"You lied, Ma," I remember repeating one particular evening as we were driven home after a family movie night. I was insistent. I needed to see a display of remorse. My mother—her eyes dutifully upon the road ahead—was only hissing at me to shut my mouth up at this point. I was seated directly behind her and her anger seeped through the back of her skull. But I was angry too. She broke the rules. We were on our way home from "The Wiz," the remake of the all-white "Wizard of Oz," starring Diana Ross, Michael Jackson, Nipsey Russell and a big brown man in a lion costume easin' on down a dirty yellow brick road. The audience seemed to enjoy it all right up to the end, but I hadn't really seen it. Only that lie before the lights went out and the movie was projected on screen, that lie while the soundtrack grooved, that lie as I was being yanked with the rest of my siblings back to the car in the night that'd befallen Brooklyn outside the local discount theater.

Chris, Angie, and Mark were a stack of arms and torsos fallen asleep upon each other on the opposite side of the rear seat, their mouths suckling breath. I slid my cheek against the glass on my side of the car. Outside was all movement and repetition as each street light streamed by, both cause and effect. But all I knew for certain was my preadolescent sense of violation, the coolness of the glass on my face, and the inertia carrying our banana-yellow 1973 Pontiac back to a man who would hold onto it long after its skin had begun to brown. My father kept it parked in front of our building where the rest of us watched it overtaken with rust until it was easier for him to pay 40-something dollars a month to keep it in the parking lot on the next block down Lincoln Place owned by the Puerto Rican lady. That Pontiac sat corroding in that lot for another couple of years before he finally let it go. My father was really stubborn that way. I was stubborn too.

Back home, I was shoved backwards to sit down at the sturdy little wooden desk in the bedroom the other boys and I shared. The shades in the bay windows were all pulled down. I don't know where my parents had shut away the other kids, but the only traces of life in our apartment at the point my father appeared at the door of the room were my own heartbeat and the whispering just outside the door. He was about to teach me a lesson.

I was almost twelve years old and I was convinced I was in the right on all this. Mothers don't lie—certainly not *my* mother. Those were the rules. My rules. Angie and Mark were both *over* 5 years old, yet Ma presented them to the ticket booth attendant as younger so she could purchase their tickets at the discount. They didn't even look that young! And that my own mother would do so on *purpose*…well, that was my defense anyway. Shading me from the glare of the single 60-watt ceiling bulb, my father asked me if Ma had actually **spoken** a lie to anyone about anything at all. I was caught off guard by that question, and I was surprised that it undercut my prepared argument about mothers not being liars. I could do nothing but acknowledge that my mother hadn't uttered a word to the ticket booth attendant beyond the customary "Thank you" as Ma requested her tickets. I couldn't find the language to justify my behavior.

Outmaneuvered, I suddenly had nothing more than a tiny shelf of righteous indignation remaining as a platform to stand on. So instead, I pressed myself down into the crevices of the chair I was seated in. No more rules. No more guide rails. My father reached forward and calmly removed the glasses from my face. Still puzzling over my failure to communicate and preoccupied with my search for more effective words, I didn't anticipate what was coming next because it had never happened before. I followed his hands with my eyes as he laid my glasses aside on the desk. Near-sighted, I squinted at his silhouetted figure against the bulb behind him as the blur of his right hand disappeared into a crashing thud against the left side of my face. Inertia took me on a ride as my weight was pitched backwards, muscles frozen, legs of the chair tipping with the blow, my face and inner ear numbed, optic nerves sparkling, the chair and I twisting, center of gravity tilting, all to bounce me heavily and then once again against the dull linoleum floor.

I tried to generate some errant, uncoordinated attempts to rise, but could manage no more than that. I knew I needed to get up but, tangled in the chair and stunned from the force of my father's blow, each attempt failed with me collapsing in a pile of new wreckage. My father had chosen not to pull his punch. The outside corner of my left eyelid began flickering violently and would do so from time to time for many months thereafter. In the distance, Ma's voice cried out some muffled and indiscernible words that spilled into my ears like the classic Doppler effect as she began moving in my direction from the doorway at the opposite corner of the room. I could make out her shape rushing in and out of my sightline between my father's pants legs as he continued to stand over me, completing his demonstration of the authority to put me in my place—left in a crumbled heap like Sarge always did to Army private Beetle Bailey at the end of one of Mort Walker's Sunday comic strips. Ma broke the rules again. My father's rules this time. I was supposed to remain in the pile at his feet. How else was I supposed to learn my lesson? It was Ma who gathered me up from the floor. I allowed her to hold on to me. I wanted to be held.

Not long after, I added the word ***deception*** to my vocabulary, yet another essential plate in my armored shell. Like I said, my father taught me many things, both directly and indirectly. And I've always been a quick learner.

*   *   *

Part of my armor was necessarily psychological. For example, I found it impossible to call my father "Dad." Our relationship so clipped and the intimacy of that term so inauthentic to my own internal sense of propriety, the word simply would not fall out of my mouth fully formed. I needed to maintain emotional distance from someone so close and yet so menacing. So, I developed the habit of clipping off the "d" sound at the end of the word, extending the "a" sound, and wound up calling him "Daa." That was the word that tumbled from my lips with consistency, trailing off unresolved. I was aware of all my odd habits, this one no less so than all the others. But in this case, I totally understood the origin of the behavior. To my mind, I didn't have a whole

Dad, not the Brady Bunch kind. Not the kind I could talk to the way I'd always imagined and wanted. I lived in the house of the man who fathered me and that seemed to be the extent of the relationship. Calling or responding to him on any given day always involved an emotional disconnect, a subtle stammer, a verbal symptom of my distrust and anxiety, a private rebellion. And to anyone who was really listening, it was also evidence of my own sense of loss. I had a Daa. I wanted more, but the relationship was outside of my ability to influence or control. If I ever called him "Daddy" as a toddler, I honestly do not remember it.

*   *   *

In 1991, my father was downsized by the Newspaper Advertising Bureau, the last company he worked for that provided him a regular paycheck. As was typical for him, he didn't offer any details to us kids at the time. However, I interviewed my father in January of 1998 and he finally filled in some of the blanks.

> I came from an overabundance…but not really using the most of my abilities. The last place I worked for, I was making a good salary. But it had reached a point where no one really wanted to be creative. There was merger talk and everyone was kind of playing it safe. Creatively I had reached kind of a standstill. I should have made progress from being an award-wining type designer. I was kind of doing what people wanted me to do—told me to do. I was in a position where you don't just throw away a good paying job. But that's all it was, it was just a job.

The merger and restructuring axed a number of jobs at the Newspaper Advertising Bureau, including the one my father had held on to for the money. In order to try to land on his feet and as a means of coping with his sense of not having made the most of all the abundance and talents he'd been blessed with, my father founded Jim Rolling Studios, naming himself its Creative Director. But all this meant was that he was never again able to find a salaried position that would pay him what he believed he was worth. He took free-lance jobs where he could get them but generating a steady income became a constant struggle for the final ten years of his life. Once, long after I was grown up and had left the house, my father did manage to tell me that he was proud of me. But with so little evidence of that pride while growing up at 1260 Lincoln Place, it was hard to believe such words when offered to me after my childhood had long ended. Even so, to emphasize his sincerity, he gave me a completed portrait he'd revisited, a portrait he first created when I was still a boy. In the original version my hair was painted solid black; in this newly gifted version, he created a visual metaphor for my labyrinthian and networked thought life. I think it was his way of acknowledging that I was never a "birdbrain" at all.

Long after I'd left my father's house to become a graduate student living on my own in an off-campus apartment near Syracuse University, I once had a dream and woke up from it with a revelation. In the dream, my father was a deeply wounded man. When I pieced together that dream with the very, very few unhappy stories he had told me about his childhood, it dawned on me that he had probably been brutalized himself as a boy by some of the men in his mother's life, especially by one of her male companions who was a police officer. My father barely mentioned it to me over the

years. But I do remember him saying to me once that he
wanted to kill that man. I never forgot him saying that. It
must have been pretty bad because my father said he was sent
to live in Florida for a period of time. Sadly, I now confess
there came a point as a young man when I had also sworn
to myself that if my father ever put his hands on any of us
again, I would kill him. But, after that dream, seeing him
in my mind's eye as unhealthy and weak for the first time,
I was able to pity him and make peace with his failings. I
finally figured out how to forgive him.

Since my father didn't have his father around to teach him
things, most of the things he was really good at, he taught
himself how to do—whether it was making art, paddleball,
pool, bowling, or playing chess. And he was really good at a
lot of things. In 1983, he won first place in the City Doubles
Masters of the 6th Annual NYC (Budweiser) Paddleball
Championship conducted by the NYC Department of Parks
& Recreation. One thing my father did not do well at all was
to manage his diabetes. Looking back at how his life ended,
I wrote several poems to help me process his last weeks on
earth. In one of those poems, I focused on the debris and
left-behinds I found in my father's living room after his life
ebbed away in 2002.

My Father's Wall Unit

My father's living room is unlived in anymore
the house about to be quietly sold
My father wanted it so I think

I found his mother's death certificate
in a neat pile on the front edge of the upper righthand shelf
over the bar of his funky late 1970s
faux wood laminate wall unit

The pile of aged letters was just in front
of an out-of-date set of World Book encyclopedias
just inside the upper glass doors
with the heavy magnetic latch

The certificate was stacked along with carefully kept photos
of his mother who died of cancer in 1965
when people only whispered about such things
if they thought the kids weren't paying attention

The certificate was carefully kept
along with two blue envelopes
now stained with 40 years, written by the hand of Eva B.
while still of sound mind and bed-ridden body at the time

Written lovingly to her only son
to guide the distribution of her earthly possessions
here at 1260 Lincoln Place
which we are about to sell

My father wanted to sell, I am certain

He signed the papers alone, without consultation
And a week after his signature, his body betrayed him

We used those encyclopedias to death
my father's encyclopedias
all four of his children under the weight of the expectations
of two parents who made us do our homework
before we went out to play

We used my father's encyclopedias inside his living room
on the wide oval coffee table beneath my father's wall unit
and when we finished our homework, he had us replace them
each one in its proper order
back inside his wall unit

But now the couch inside my father's living room
is dented where he slept each night
uncomfortable for years in beds
the upholstery oily with seepage from skin and wounds
the carpet embedded with the sediment of
layers of dry flaked skin

His shoes and slippers, odorous and misshapen
are collected in a black garbage bag
in the middle of that matted rust-colored carpet

Preferring to walk alone even near the end
my father walked to the recreation center
when he could no longer run the paddleball courts
he walked to the V.A. hospital
where he disagreed with Nurse Riley
on the care of his diabetic foot

an ulcer growing
my father's peculiar cancer
merciless at his heel
dogging him as he hobbled in his orthopedic boot,
or shuffled in unlaced, oversized sneakers

Sometime during his last week at 1260 Lincoln Place
as his sugar went screaming
to a final count of 628 on the blood meter
diligently recorded by his unstable hand
in a small white medical diary
in an addled script that bounced and jagged off the page
as his body cried out loud for help
still my father did not call for the hospital
did not call his children
did not call his wife or neighbors
or even Nurse Riley
until his voice was too weak to call at all
until my wife found him sitting in his urine
his back against the kitchen radiator

Perhaps he wanted it so
his word always being the last

Intubated in his final three weeks at St. Mary's Hospital
as sepsis killed organs in succession
and an ICU-borne necrosis killed flesh
he never recovered his speech
never recovered his breathing

Filling the open bar of my father's wall unit
there are white boxes instead of liquor bottles,

gauze pads, plastic containers and topical solutions
but the insulin syringes are hardly used

As I exit the living room, turning into the darkened hallway
past the cracked green ceramic lamp with the broken switch
the lamp we can finally throw away

I know I am leaving the scene of an accident that waited

Waited

Knowing him, I think he wanted it so

*   *   *

Sometime after my father died at 3:49 PM on July 8, 2002 at the age of 63 due to diabetes-related complications, a group of men he had known for fifteen years showed up at his wake, prior to the funeral. I had not met any of them before and would not see them again after that day. But I found out that these gentlemen who had come to honor my dead father used to play chess in the local parks with him on a regular basis. My father was a self-taught chess player. They told me they'd nicknamed him "Nemesis" because no matter how hard they tried to defend their queen, they could not escape his dogged maneuvers across the chessboard. Yes, my father won his share of local tournament trophies for his chess-playing skills, but most of the time he played out of his unspoken internal drive to achieve and control and leave his own mark on the world even if no one else saw it.

As James Haywood Rolling, Jr., I can't escape my father

either. Like him, I don't share emotions well. Like him, I am private to a fault. Like him, when I've wanted to achieve or attain or accomplish a thing, I've taught myself how to do it. Often too slowly for my own satisfaction I confess, but eventually. Deliberately. I'm sure I also learned my persistence from him. Those are the rules.

Eulogy and Ambiguity

After opening my dad's armoire
in the curtained art studio in the back room of the house
and upon discovery of his updated resume
hidden in his last portfolio
out of circulation
a decade after he was downsized
daily updating his design skills for a computer age
that was no longer willing to pay him a salary

after compiling achievements stamped in peeling metal
dated labels at the bases of tarnished tournament prizes
armless trophy men that once held silver racquets
and broken chess pieces that once held crowns

after examining 30 years
packed into two drawers
records and receipts, stack against stack
composed with the same care as his color palettes

I have evidence to write in praise of

a typographer awarded for his hand-drawn letters

an illustrator whose beginner's math book was read in China

an author whose memoirs were never published

a poet honorably mentioned by Reader's Digest

found in the ruins of his fallen castles
the wreckage of two generations at 1260 Lincoln Place
where firstborn James's were given no berth to speak
their love of fathers or hatred of hardened men

In the end he said he was proud of me
went into his art studio in the back room of the house
and tried to unpack 30 years of distance and hesitancy
into a portrait of me as his creation

5

asthma

Reading to myself about ants and bees in the
hallway of our second-floor apartment.

THE FIRST COLLEGE CLASSROOM I ever stood in was at
Long Island University just after I had started elementary
school. I was essentially a "show-and-tell" display. My
older cousin David, also a visual artist, wanted to refute an
argument leveled during a "nature vs. nurture" debate in one
of his classes. It had been asserted that a youngster growing
up like I did, in a lower-income and predominantly African
American neighborhood in Brooklyn, was highly unlikely

to fulfill any potential for individual achievement in equal
measure to that of a child growing up in an educationally
nurturing, middle class environment. My cousin David
believed I was gifted and knew that the nurturing of teachers
had not been required to produce me. He simply asked me
to bring in my artwork and the richly detailed stories that
always accompanied each cross-section of an underground
colony or space station I drew in my spare time, and to talk
about my drawings with his college classmates.

I was too young at the time to recall now if David
changed any minds that day, but I vividly remember his classmates, all white, prompting me with question after question.
I also recall the strange sense that they'd never had a close
encounter before with a boy who looked and talked like
me. I know for sure I enjoyed their attention. It made me
feel safe. Throughout my childhood and adolescent years, I
taught myself numerous ways to feel safe. For as long as I
could remember, I felt safest keeping my thoughts to myself.
I didn't have an interest in investing the time to make a lot of
friends because I was already preoccupied with things other
kids typically expressed no interest in. I loved noticing things
that nobody else seemed to give a second glance. Sitting
outside within the confines of our sidewalk gate, I used to
closely observe bees slowly hovering in circles around the rose
bush we'd planted in the front yard, or the processions of
ants marching in and out of cracks between the steps leading
down to the cellar door beneath our front stoop. From my
second-floor bedroom window, I catalogued everything from
insects landing on the sill, to kids at play, to teens hanging
out, to adults walking by, to raindrops falling in heavy wind-
swept sheets gusting one by one down Lincoln Place. Yet
while it may have seemed to outside observers that it was my

social anxieties and distancing that most defined me, I knew that my asthma and the allergies that triggered them had a huge role in shaping my cautious approach to the world.

I have had allergies to grass, pollen, cigarette smoke, and house dust for as long as I can remember. For several years, my mother regularly took me to Dr. Sabrkesh with his office in an apartment building that had its own doorman at the other end of Eastern Parkway, at Grand Army Plaza near Prospect Park, where lots of wealthy white folks still lived. Dr. Sabrkesh was a specialist in pediatric allergies and he had me on a regimen of shots every few weeks that were intended to introduce small doses of allergens into my body to gradually increase my tolerance and lessen the adverse effects of each triggering encounter. Since I still suffer from reactions to all of those very same allergens, I can't say that any of this worked. But the severity of my misery made the effort to diminish it worth a try. I do remember how the final shot in each regimen always felt like I had just been suddenly kicked in the arm by a horse on top of the sudden swelling at the site of the inoculation.

I had my first full-blown asthma attack when I was 8 or 9 years old. I think the trigger was breathing a heavy concentration of the fumes of bathroom detergents like Lysol or Pine-Sol while I was washing the bathroom floor. As was my habit, I did not tell my parents I needed their help or that I was struggling to breathe. I attempted to handle the problem myself. As I wheezed and struggled to fill my lungs with air, I remember the intuition I had to sit myself still near an open window, to calm and slow my breathing, and to drink a cup of warm water. No one knew yet that I had inherited my grandmother's asthma, not even me. Eventually, I began to cough up the mucous that was clogging me. While I may

have spent an hour or so struggling to breathe, my asthma
is considered mild. I've never needed to be hospitalized. But
after the muscular exertion of struggling to overcome an
asthma attack, I was always overcome with the need to take a
deep nap and hit the reset button.

Playing outdoors during the explosion of tree pollen
on an early Spring day or ragweed pollens in the Fall could
trigger my asthma. Exposure to air pollution in the crowded
city could trigger my asthma. Being around cats and dogs,
especially in rooms with carpeting and no ventilation, could
trigger my asthma. Exerting myself in cold weather, whether
playing handball or shoveling snow, could trigger my asthma.
Being in my dusty house doing any kind of household
cleaning, from sweeping the floor to washing out the tub
with Mr. Clean or Pine-Sol, could trigger my asthma. Being
around cigarette smokers, as most of my cousins were, could
trigger my asthma. I learned to be careful. I learned to remove
myself. In school, however, there were no triggers for my
asthma attacks at all and that made it a sanctuary. For that
reason alone, I rarely missed a day of school.

By midday at P.S. 52 in Sheepshead Bay, the bell would
typically have sounded, signaling lunchtime recess. Kids,
slow at first, then thick, emptied into the schoolyard, an
open court partitioned with fencing and canopied by a
borderline of old trees, their muscular roots pushing up from
the ground in gnarled knots resembling huge, calloused toe
knuckles, splitting and disheveling the uniformity of the
sidewalk slabs surrounding their thick trunks. First in slow
dribbles, then rushing through metal doors like timed inci-
sions in the cinderblock, children gushed out into the yard,
pooling into groups according to grade level and gender to
collapse Indian-legged near piles of shed jackets and sweaters

to start eating. There was a tumult of hinged metal lunch-boxes opening all at once and then the smell of soggy Wonder bread, peanut butter and jelly, warm ham sandwiches in plastic wrap, potato chips in Baggies, and cold hotdogs in crunched up aluminum foil. There were clattering thermos caps, crumbled animal crackers, shoe shuffles, screaming giggles, spilt milk, and a hundred metallic rips of unzipping zippers. Recess was a sanctioned frenzy.

Still being in the early 1970s, the genders parted once we entered the schoolyard. Fourth and fifth grade girls came together into clusters of skirts and dresses, playing jump rope or jacks, moving in and out and about each other like painted horses on a spinning carousel. The older boys gathered on the other side of a dividing fence in an area with a painted base path where they played punchball and dodgeball, battled, tugged, and wrestled, indulging in *Cracked* and *MAD Magazine*, flashing biceps or one another's trading cards, or showing off the latest Marvel or DC comics purchases in their plastic collectable sleeves. My asthma always restricted me from running freely like the others, whether around diamonds or in circles or dashing across rectangles. But my isolation on the playground wasn't just from my own sense of caution. I was also one of only a handful of Black children at P.S. 52. In every one of my classrooms, I was usually the only one. I was never made to feel welcomed at the center of any activity. I was treated like a peripheral concern by most of the teachers in the building.

Imperfect as they were in changing times, my adult tether lines throughout elementary school were my first through fifth grade homeroom teachers, Mrs. Erenrich, Mrs. Licht, Mrs. Zivin, Mrs. Finkelstein, and Mrs. Greer, all of whom dutifully recorded my grades and my escalating reading

placement scores for each year's grade report. But they were
never quite able to bridge the social chasm between me and
their other students as the only Black boy in their classroom.
How many times did they not even bother to help me comb
my hair for the annual class photographs? I have the evidence.
Yet at the close of my first-grade school year, my teacher, Mrs.
Erenrich, gave me one of the most life-changing gifts I've ever
received. The simplest of gifts, she gave me books to read over
the summer. She let me select each one, books that plugged
me in and turned the engine on, not just because of the additional reading but because of the thoughtful act. She had
been paying attention after all. She had noticed how deeply I
immersed myself when reading. I only fully remember a few
of the book titles, from *Curious George* to *Ants and Bees*. The
latter book on the hidden life of insects had cross-sectional
drawings of the architecture hidden inside of a typical underground ant colony and a beehive, reminding me that much
of what was inside my head remained as invisible to everyone
else as my asthma.

From the summer after first grade through the remainder
of my elementary schooling, my love of books continued to
fill the voids left by my interpersonal detachments. Contra-
dicting the popular stereotypes that rendered me either flat,
dull, and stupid or a dangerous additive to neighborhoods
like Sheepshead Bay, I was a regular in the school library,
reading about dolphins and panthers and saber-tooth tigers,
Encyclopedia Brown the boy detective, and science fiction
adventurer Danny Dunn. But, books weren't the only fuel
for my earliest creative leaps. Oh, the sights to be seen on my
way to school each morning! Through my rattling school bus
window, I watched a theatrical display of architectural tran-
sitions parade from stage left to stage right—from the dingy

familiarity of the apartment buildings in Crown Heights
to the vividness of neighborhoods over which I claimed
ownership by right of my painstaking observation.

Day by day, I catalogued free-standing homes that
strangely did not share each other's walls, homes surrounded
instead by front yards and back yards or whole plots of land,
often accented with above-ground swimming pools painted
blue, sporting driveways and carports addressing two-car
garages. There were two-story Mike and his Brady Bunch
structures with jutting rooftops and parental Norway maples
and London planetrees hugging their eaves in affectionate
greenery; there were oak trees with rope swings lashed to their
boughs, some with treehouses swaddled in their branches.

As our yellow school bus entered these neighborhoods, I
liked to unlatch the window beside my seat so that it slapped
down a few notches and I could breathe in the aromas of
passing trees, tucking me back into my seat with a blanket of
fresh oxygen that soothed all my asthmas. And the holidays!
There were great peeling trunks of trees, foreign to Lincoln
Place, dumping bark and thick color onto lawns like gener-
ously inked Charles Schulz's Sunday "Peanuts" comic panels
come to life. I would imagine Schroeder's fingers racing at the
keyboards playing jazz riffs for Charlie Brown's other friends
to dance to. I saw jack-o-lanterns and other orange and
brown paraphernalia nailed to doorways, skeletons lashed
to fences, ghosts along the rooftop overhangs, paper turkeys
and Pilgrims on porches, twisted gourds and copious woven
baskets stacked with dried ears of multi-colored kernelled
corn. And in the final months of the year, I committed to
memory street after street of white unstained snow with
strings of light taut against the early winter light, wrapping
roofs and windows with competing displays of dispensable

income—the reddish glow of countless plastic Santa Clauses
and blinking reindeer noses marching around and above
those unapproachable houses. I committed these sights to
memory not knowing I would write about them decades
later. I needed to remember there were always alternatives to
1260 Lincoln Place.

On pleasantly chilled Fall afternoons when we were still
allowed outside at lunchtime for recess in snug bubble jackets
and thickening sweaters, even while other kids shrieked and
laughed and dodged and ran, my mind would begin to drift
elsewhere in daydream. After I had eaten, I would often lay my
Scooby-Doo lunchbox down beside the tall fence to further
inspect the area through my small black-rimmed glasses.
Roaming up and down along the schoolyard's perimeter
with my fingertips skipping slowly across the cold metal
links, I crunched my way through drying layers of leaves that
were still changing color even after they had dropped to the
ground. It would often occur to me to select from among
fat acorns the biggest and best of the fallen shapes carpeted
across my exploring feet. With great care, I would tear and
pinch and fold back the pointed lobes of my favorites of all
the leaves I'd collected. And when I had finally shaped my
finest fleet of spaceships, I would launch myself from beneath
the shelter of high oak trees, to conquer blue worlds of my
own creation.

*   *   *

By the end of each day, I'd always observed a great deal—
all while keeping a safe distance. That way, whatever was
wrong with me was also kept far from view. I wasn't used
to much physical contact at all. I have no warm childhood

memories of being embraced or snuggled or rocked to sleep while curled up in the arms of my parents. Ma was more physically affectionate with my younger siblings and I always suspected it was because I was a living reminder of her most painful childbirth. My father typically kept to himself, unless he was doling out discipline that wasn't intended to mold me, but rather to break me. If I was touched as a boy, it was usually in the form of punishment. And because I was the oldest child, when I got punished I always got it the worst— often for things that were hard to control, like, not getting the younger kids into bed by the time my parents got home from a night out. I got pounded by my father for that once.

To be honest, I got whooped for whatever offended my father's sense of order or that lacked what he had predetermined as simple "common sense." One day, Ma made us all some hamburgers, with a slice of tomato. I was always a picky eater and the taste of biting into the raw tomato made me gag involuntarily. I said I couldn't eat it, but my father insisted I could if I really wanted to. I did not answer back, of course. And while I did eat everything else on the plate, I had such a hard time forcing that tomato down, I made the mistake of leaving it for last. As usual, my father accused me of being stubborn. But that day he lost his temper with unusual abandon and he grabbed up a nearby broomstick. Without holding back, he beat me down with that broomstick until I was wedged in the back corner of our small kitchen, between the radiator and its locked rear door, trying unsuccessfully to escape his blows. When his rage had passed, my father sat me back at the table to finish eating that cold slice of tomato— which I promptly retched back up onto the plate.

Eventually, I taught myself not to cry when being brutalized like that—the same way I had taught myself not to crack a smile when I was a little boy, thinking I was just the ugliest thing. I'm not sure if it was because of lessons he'd learned from surviving his own childhood or surviving boot camp training from his years in the Army, but it was only when I finally stopped showing any reaction at all to his beatings and was able to silently endure his hardest swings that my father stopped hitting me so frequently.

a failure of imagination

Who knew that hope evacuates the pores of the young
like the onset of a fresh wave of asthma
withering my imagination
left dry as driftwood
and my lungs gasping for creation?

Who knew that hope abandons the heart
like the slow evaporation
of those earliest waters that sustained me
eroding the stories I'd first lived by
leaching desert canyons in the soul?

Who knew I could not compel the release
of hope's terraforming flood
no matter my thirst for words or expression
no matter how parched and broken the earth
or how much I'd prayed for rain from any direction?

Still I pray

no matter the shape
of whatever cloud comes
or how thin the vapor
that falls to fill
the drought-cloven scars
in this human clay

I pray

6.

predatory behavior

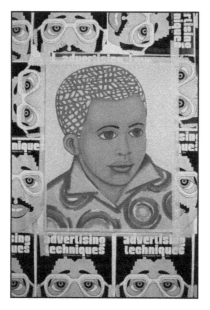

Detail of a work of art I created to depict my
dread about being cornered by my father.

THE BEHAVIOR OF PREDATORS varies depending on what
they're hunting. I've encountered two kinds of predatory
behavior. Typically, most predators go after other species—
crocodiles ambushing gazelles at the local watering hole, for
example, or a pack of wolves identifying a weak or sickly
buffalo and ganging up on it to bring it down from the rear.

This is one kind of predatory behavior. But on some rare occasions, predators have been known to kill and eat their own offspring. It's hard to know what triggers this second kind of predatory behavior—sometimes the trigger is a desperate lack of nourishment, sometimes its competition for habitat or control over the local gene pool, and sometimes it's just the predator's basic instinct gone awry.

From the time I started first grade, my parents had bused all of us kids from the Rolling household to Sheepshead Bay, way on the other end of the borough of Brooklyn where the neighborhoods were mostly white. They wanted us to go to a better school than what they knew was available in our own neighborhood. They wanted us all to go to college knowing that kids who went to school in our neighborhood often barely finished high school.

In the first grade, while riding the bus to school, a little white boy named Thomas used to sit behind me from the time he got on the bus until we made it to P.S. 52. During the ride, Thomas liked to comb his pale little fingers through the tight black coils of my hair. My head must have seemed otherworldly to him. Frankly, I really didn't mind the odd intimacy of having my scalp caressed. At least having my hair messed up was a better form of attention than the dirty thumbtacks a couple of bullies regularly hid on my seats as we moved from classroom to classroom, puncturing my flesh when I least expected it.

I got picked on at school and in my neighborhood for all the obvious reasons. It's easiest, perhaps, to hurt the person you don't know. It's even easier to hurt the kid who stays quiet. I was both incomprehensible and unexpressive. Nearsighted and needing to wear glasses for as long as I can remember, it's not surprising that I ended up with a few other nicknames besides Jim-Jim. Because other kids saw me as bookish and brainy and a misfit, I was also taunted with names like "Poindexter," the nerdy character with thick spectacles from the cartoon *Felix the Cat*. Or "Professor," the character from the TV show *Gilligan's Island*. Or "Spock," the alien from the popular TV series *Star Trek*. While the other nicknames were annoying or amusing, I was secretly proud of my association with Mr. Spock. I admired his control over his emotions, especially in the midst of danger. And I had a lean physique, just like Spock, who hailed from the fictional, higher-gravity planet of Vulcan. Despite his skinny frame, Spock possessed three times the strength of an average human being. I identified with the fact that Spock was easy to underestimate by his outward appearances alone. Moreover, since Spock was half-human, normal human emotions were always there beneath the surface but they rarely ever overwhelmed him. I admired Spock's ability to control his emotions. First Officer Spock was a man of action, not reaction, and that's who I wanted to be too.

There was a point in grade school when I was bullied almost daily by the other James in my class, a boy whose last name was Wolfe—quite appropriately, given his predatory behavior. I suppose he sensed weakness in me, flaws and vulnerability that made me easy prey. It was easy for him to stalk me since I only had a handful of friends in school, none of whom could defend me. Distant from everyone, I suffered his harassment in silence. I tried to avoid the boy, but he was in my classes. He would hit me, poke me, pick at me, push me, laugh at me, insult me, and torment me in any way he could get away with. I honestly didn't know what to do about it.

While I knew what it was to be bullied, I couldn't generate enough emotion to work up any kind of response at all—least of all an angry one. I had limited my give-and-take with other people so thoroughly, I had no real experience with putting up a fight. This meant my tormentor had his way with me for a long time—until one day in third grade when my anguish had finally built up enough pressure to suddenly burst into retribution. I didn't want to feel trapped anymore. It was during library period, and Mrs. White was supervising. I was sitting alone, reading in a corner of the library, when Wolfe approached. I don't remember what new injury ignited me. A punch? A pinch? But my reaction shocked even me, who'd always been self-contained and unfamiliar with self-defense. I only recall what happened next in flashes of memory: I leapt from my seat to counterattack my attacker. I pounced, full-on, with all my strength. Wolfe flopped down into a ball beneath me, with his hands and arms protecting his head. Both my fists beat down on his back in a rhythm that punctuated each syllable of my loud, vocal demand that he, "LEAVE-ME-A-LONE! LEAVE-ME-A-LONE!"

I was still pounding away and shouting at him when I slowly remembered there were other people in the library. I glanced up to see that all my classmates had moved out of their seats to bunch together at Mrs. White's desk alongside one wall of the room. They were just staring. Not one of the spectators said a word—not even Mrs. White who stood with them. But I could read sympathy in her eyes, framed by the bangs of her short black hair. More vividly than anything else, I remember how her eyes seemed to grant me her unspoken approval to do battle. In those few seconds that stretched out like minutes, she made no move to stop me. So, I focused again on battering Wolfe's body—until my explosion burnt itself out. I can't remember receiving any warnings, reprimands, or penalties for my action that day. I think my father was quietly pleased when he learned I had whooped a kid who was picking on me in school. None of my classmates treated me any differently after that incident. Even Wolfe avoided me for a while. I suspected that a lot of people in our school thought it was high time for the class bully to catch a beating. Soon thereafter, the very next time he tried to target me, I punched him in the nose without hesitation. I was promptly sent to the principal's office. Wolfe never bothered me again after that.

*   *   *

As in the natural world, there are consequences to any human behavior. For most of the years I lived at 1260 Lincoln Place, I felt like the gazelle at the water hole, never ever able to let down my guard in the presence of my father. Danger was always lurking. This should not have been so. My father's upbringing was not dissimilar to my own, fraught with unspoken pain and powers of observation most people did not share, evident at an early age. I once interviewed my father in 1998 as part of a college art assignment exploring his identity as an artist since he was a child—an identity I had also developed on my own at a similar age. If there is such a thing as a genetic mutation that predisposes a person to become an artist, I had obviously inherited my mutation from my father. From the following piece of transcript he was clearly a daydreamer long before I was. I was his first child. I should not have been under stress every day just to avoid becoming his prey.

Q: Tell me a story of an experience you had when you were raised that shows how much your life has changed since then?

A: Well, at first there were no televisions...only radios. Since I was an only child and my mother worked, [if] her boyfriend wasn't around I had to come straight home from school and stay in the house all by myself until someone came home. And by then I couldn't go out, because it was late. So I just had the radio to listen to. So the radio...a lot of things are in your imagination. There's nothing visually to see. Each person kind of imagines what the characters look like and what's happening.

Q: How are things different now?

A: When [we] moved to Brownsville [in Brooklyn], my grandmother was the first one on the block to get a TV. Sid Caesar's "Your Show of Shows," Milton Berle...when they were on, everyone on the block, on those days, would come upstairs to our house to watch TV. That's when things started to change. TV brought people together and then you could see what people were talking about. So that was the start of being visual [for me].

Q: What is the earliest art experience you can remember?

A: I used to draw from comic books and I used to collect comic books. At the time I was 6 years old [in 1944 and 1945], I used to copy comic book art. I started with Mickey Mouse, Donald Duck...Walt Disney Comics [originally published starting in 1940]. So my visual thing, up until TV, was whatever I created or saw. My mother, grandmother, [and] certain relatives would praise me and say, "That's good." They praised me as an artist even though I was just learning to be an artist. The drawings I did on my own. I was also exposed to music. One of my uncles, [a music teacher], sort of forced it on me…and that kind of made me realize that you can't force people to do things, because sometimes it'll turn into something they might not even like. You have to kind of let them find their way. By the time I was 6 years old, I decided I was going to be an artist because that's something that I did that a lot of people didn't do…people praised me and said I did it well.

Why then did my father fail to apply these very same lessons to me? Why did he spend so much time forcing things on me? Why did he spend so little time offering me HIS praise, since I was clearly so much like him? Was it because he grew up with only female role models offering him such praise? Or was it because the boyfriends in his mother's life did and said unspeakable things when his mother wasn't home? Honestly, I don't know. What I DO know is how violated I felt being forced on a regular basis to spread Pond's cold cream all over his wide back after he took a shower, as he sat facing away from me on the edge of the bathtub, naked except for his tighty-whitey Fruit of the Looms and a towel on his lap. I HATED that I could not tell him NO, I did not want to do this, that no child should be asked to do this. I HATED the texture of his bare skin under my hands. He always waited until just the right opportunity to corner me and lock me in the bathroom with him. I HATED being forced to do something I hated doing. And I hated HIM for forcing me—fully aware I was too small and voiceless to stop him from doing whatever he wanted to do to me, or even dare saying no to whatever he wanted me to do to him in his house at 1260 Lincoln Place.

battlegrounds and backdrops

the lighting's out of place
the blood isn't fake

maybe I'm an actor
it's hard to tell when the scenery is real

a person dies and everyone says
how he lived his life his way
until the end of the play
closing the curtain on his act

corpses party in clubs every night
to escape the stench of their own decay

the bullies are taken off stage
but the stains in the carpet just won't wash away

7

seen and unseen

Straining not to smile, defying
what the school photographer
had just asked me to do.

WHEN I WAS VERY young, I discovered I had pareidolia. While I confess this was a word I would only encounter in a dictionary for the first time as an adult many years after first experiencing this perceptual ability, even without knowing what this superpower was called, it was nevertheless unmistakable. Oddly, my pareidolia always insinuated itself when least expected, manifesting without any effort on my part, and typically when I had nothing much on my mind. I had

always been a careful observer, obsessively *reading* pictures
rather than merely looking at them. My ability to focus even
as a child was intense. However, because of my pareidolia
I often saw faces and figures where I didn't expect them,
allowing me to find clarity and recognition in the most
vague and indistinct surface patterns. I typically saw faces
that emerged unexpectedly from their backgrounds. Human
portraits. Wild animals. Imaginary creatures. My pareidolia
would allow me to suddenly see faces in the torn linoleum
flooring in the apartment where I grew up. They would pop
up in the grains of wood and the cracks of ceiling plaster. I
would notice them outside in the shapes of crushed autumn
leaves or in stains on the sidewalk. Sometimes the faces and
torsos were amusing caricatures, sometimes grotesque, sometimes in perfect proportion. I was surrounded by faces all
throughout my childhood. These weren't hallucinations at
all. Rather, they were right there in the gritty details. I never
looked for them—they just became apparent and I received
them as new perceptions. Anomalies within preexisting
structures. Possibilities. Reinterpretations. Unhidden and
recognized for the first time by anyone's eyes. By my super-
powered eyes.

*   *   *

I have worn glasses constantly since I was nine years old.
My eyes aren't close to normal. The stars in the night sky
are no more than a soupy blur to my faulty eyes without
performance-enhancing lenses. I have progressive myopia
along with an astigmatism, the latter being a defect in the
spherical curvature of my eyes that prevents light from
focusing properly on my retinas. Yet along with my extreme

nearsightedness, the general weakness of my eyes has always seemed to heighten my awareness of what I *am* able to see. Like the David Dunn, the security guard character played by Bruce Willis in the M. Night Shyamalan film *Unbreakable*, I discovered other superpowers as I came of age.

One was my ability to hide in plain sight. Hiding my smile and retaining all my emotions behind hard shell walls had unexpected consequences. During my ugliest years as a little boy, if the whole family had gathered to watch some laugh-out-loud show on TV in the living room, I would usually watch from the shadows just out in the hallway, positioning myself with the stealth of a housecat, swallowing my laughter and pushing it back down my own throat. Controlling what I had control over. I wanted to believe no one knew I was right outside the doorway. But no one's that good at remaining hidden.

It's more likely that my parents knew of my odd and compulsive behavior but just didn't know what to do with me. If my mother or father did happen to notice me in the hallway or incidentally brushed past as I concealed myself in the dark of the hallway—paralyzed with low self-esteem and debating whether I wanted to enter and show myself in the light or not—one or the other of them usually asked me to come into the living room. I usually declined. They knew they couldn't force me to come in. And we all knew I had grown more comfortable in my self-seclusion than in the company of my own family.

At Christmas time, I also preferred my solitude over the company of family gatherings. Because my birthday is on December 28, just three days after the hustle and bustle of Christmas day, there were even two or three years where my family lost track of my upcoming birthday and I ended up with more than a few make-up presents! To be fair, there was a lot going on for everyone during the holidays. Too much for me. So, every year I collected all of my presents from under the tree, took them to my room, closed the door, and opened my gifts in silence and the absence of the unwelcome pressure of onlookers waiting for my emotional responses. If I ripped away the wrapping paper in front of others, I would be expected to smile. Honestly, I had forgotten how to feel comfortable with a smile on my face. I know for sure that my family thought this behavior was strange because I *also* thought it was strange. But I was at a point where I could no longer help myself. While I didn't want to behave this way, I also did not know how to feel or act "normal." And I had no one I could talk with about how to make the strangeness go away, even in my own home.

Then, again, it wasn't my home. My father used to declare, routinely, that 1260 Lincoln Place was *his* house. And we all knew he meant exactly what he said. To make this point clear to everyone, he made sure his name alone was on the property deed. Ma thought that was unfair and asked more than once for her name to be added to the deed. But my father wouldn't budge. As for me, I just bided my time in his house, hidden. Unseen.

*   *   *

The other major superpower I discovered was my ability to absorb music. I love to sing. It corrects me. I graduated from P.S. 52 in June of 1974 not only with an Honor Award for "Attendance," but with an Honor Award for "Excellence in Music - Chorus." At night, I'd often take a small radio to bed with me. At that age, I favored pop songs by artists like Elton John, Stevie Wonder, Barry Manilow, Roberta Flack,

Billy Joel, or Donny Hathaway, all singing words that I wished were my own. Whenever I happened to be in the house alone during the daytime, there were certain album recordings I would carefully pull from my father's vinyl collection to replay over and over again on his living room stereo turntable—typically the songs that made me cry or that made the hairs stand up on my arms and the back of my neck. I always made sure to put back whichever album I'd selected *exactly* where I found it, between the two other albums where my father had originally slotted it so he would have no evidence it had ever been moved at all. I would re-listen to these rare songs I discovered were able to penetrate my castle-walled emotional defenses only when I was alone in the house—usually with the curtains drawn, the lights dimmed low, and the sound cranked up high enough to overwhelm my bulwarked senses. I freely admit, I welcomed such invasions.

One such song was titled "Everything Must Change," originally written and debuted by Benard Ighner as a guest vocalist on the 1974 Quincy Jones studio jazz album, *Body Heat*. By opening the castle gates to such invasions, I tended to the wounds of my adolescence as a deliberate means of altering the inertia that kept me isolated and ineffectual as a human being. I knew I wanted to live a meaningful life, but I was just as aware that I could not do so unless I learned to share what was hidden within me as directly as these songs did. Songs like Stevie Wonder's "Living for the City" from his 1973 *Innervisions* album—drum riffs and synthesizers echoing through the same-old same-old, ripping away the monotony, and pulsing across my mind and spirit like a warming balm applied to an injury. Ighner's song has been covered by numerous artists, from Nina Simone to George Benson to Oleta Adams, but the lyrics always begin this way:

Everything must change
Nothing stays the same
Everyone must change
No one stays the same

The young become the old
And mysteries do unfold
Cause that's the way of time
Nothing and no one goes unchanged

There are not many things in life
You can be sure of
Except rain comes from the clouds
Sun lights up the sky
And hummingbirds do fly

Some people self-harm themselves, something I've never done. The reasons vary. Some people cut themselves to distract themselves when they're feeling overwhelmed. Some cut themselves to release the tension of intense emotions. Some people cut themselves just to feel something, anything, when they've been numbed by the severity of their circumstances. Music works the same way for me. It cuts me open. But it never harms me; it heals. It releases. Ighner concludes the song "Everything Must Change" with a verse that actually explains not only my need, but my love for music and its ability to open me up:

Rain comes from the clouds
Sun lights up the sky
And music
And music
Makes me cry

Not everything changed. I was still human, no changing that. The display of any emotion, even crying, is a social cue to behave and emote likewise. I didn't follow those cues when prompted. Since I'm human, and all humans need to vent their emotions at some point or another, always containing my emotions hurt me more than it did anyone else. Nevertheless, even though I had a lot to cry about on any given day, I simply did not. Not in front of people though. Instead, I'd replay a song that made me cry again and again, alone in the dark behind curtains. Or I'd listen to those songs on the radio at night under a tented sheet pulled taut over my raised knees and propped up head. I did that more than anyone knew. Unseen.

*   *   *

My greatest superpower of all is my ability to make something from nothing. To make something visible that was not there before. When I was a child, I discovered I was a part of an ancient secret society—a society of mutants with the ability to take blank white pages and turn them into stories, characters, fantasies, and pictures that simply would not leave your thinking. I learned how to read our society's creative codes—in pen and ink or with splashes of color—and recode them as my own. I discovered the existence of this society while mining deep into my father's closet of black plastic garbage bags filled with vintage Marvel and DC comics featuring stories of other superheroes like me, tales from the crypt, and the escapades of Archie, Betty, Veronica, Jughead and the gang. I introduced myself to even more members of our secret society as I paged through the collected anthologies that lined my father's art studio bookshelves, compilations of the life's work of artists ranging from Charles Schulz, the creator of *Peanuts*—to the soothingly dark, macabre worlds of artists like Charles Addams and Edward Gorey—to the obscure illustrators of risqué pulp advertisements and girlie drawings who sought to either titillate the repressed Main Streets of the 1950s, or surf the waves of countercultural 1960s Americana.

While I discovered my creative superpower in my father's art studio, it took years of development to learn to use my powers for good, typically by drawing a new face from time to time to add to the gallery of faces I already saw in the world. In other words, I became a portrait artist. Creating a portrait is not a magic trick; it is a craft, a commitment to gathering up the resources at hand, assembling them, and then giving my best away. For years I've found myself drawn to the challenge of taking either the photograph or the reality of an individual sitting before me, and reconstructing the life I perceive behind their eyes. What I will eventually render is not exactly as it appears. It doesn't have to be. My commitment to the reinterpretation of a life is what matters. My favorite method is to begin with a black & white photograph of the subject. In so doing, I begin my search for color and life as through a cloak of varying grays. My understanding of the life in front of me begins with nothing but a sketch. Life is reconstructed layer by layer. From which direction is the light cast? At what point will I notice and repair my initial misalignments? Nostrils too wide. Correction. An ear lobe too low. Adjustment. The left eyebrow arched at too acute an angle. Reshape it. Then, a skin color is invented, or rather, a mixture of light and dark colors that don't seem at first to belong together. Then I add gradations to those colors, ever-softened gradations, blended and combined. The portrait comes to life in the process of creation. And my eye is always enthralled as life rises to the surface of the canvas or illustration board.

In the end, a portrait never seems finished until I see it leap to life. I've been known to work for 8 hours straight on a portrait without a break as the image is refined. I've also been known to start working again on a portrait years after I initially started it. Until it makes itself seen. Until the eyes finally make me cry.

music from the main lodge

In a hard, orange chair
under dawning summer sun
in the middle of a meadow of grass

hills to the front of me
a flagpole on my left
campgrounds woven with fully green trees

behind me, from the main lodge
the sound system is loud,
filling my head with animations of song

twisting awkward through time
busting open gateways
of black, wrought iron teenaged emotion

8

lost & found

Me and my siblings in the living room as
I was doing homework.

MA ONCE TOLD ME she was in labor with me for a full 12
hours as I stubbornly insisted on entering the world butt-
first, until I was finally turned around by the doctors so I

could be born in a more reasonable fashion. She said her last three emerged with far less difficulty—Chris was born three years after me, Mark three years after Chris, and Angie in between Chris and Mark. Nevertheless, and apparently in spite of the considerable pain I caused her, Ma gifted me with flash cards and used them with me very early on in my literacy development as a regular means to drill word and pattern recognition into my perception. My literacy was further stimulated because of my parents' decision to enroll me in a community pre-kindergarten class. I keep an album with my school photos from over the years and my pre-kindergarten class photo depicts the only level of education I've ever experienced where, except for the one single happy white child at the end of my row, I am surrounded by a classroom full of smiling Black children with two African American co-teachers—a man and a woman, whose names I have no record of.

While it might seem I was unhappy throughout most of my childhood, that actually wasn't the case. Certain activities and observations brought me great joy and fascination. Art brought me tremendous joy, and still does. In fact, making art made me smart. Immersing myself in art and visual storytelling also made me curious about almost everything and drove my desire to excel at whatever I put my mind to. I enjoyed making sense of the world, one bit and one subject at a time. In school, I never let myself get bored. I persistently asked questions. I learned fast. I was a black boy, accelerated. From elementary school on, I consistently tested several grades or more ahead of the expected reading level for my age group. By the time I was in middle school, my reading level was testing out somewhere in the vicinity of a typical eleventh or twelfth grader.

Thinking set me free from feeling. Studying, and sometimes just wondering, allowed me to take mental strolls in the park, away from the unpleasant reality of way too many circumstances beyond my control. Yet even as I observed life either from inside a shell or through a distant telescope, I retained and could recall much of the information I encountered. Never being bored has its advantages. But while old report cards of mine show evidence of outstanding grades over the years, they also tell another story. Yes, I was the nerdy kid who read dictionaries and encyclopedia entries for fun. But I was also regularly reprimanded for daydreaming, given that I often became more interested in imagining what was happening just beyond the nearest classroom window than paying attention to what was happening inside. Whatever I missed, I knew I'd catch up fast.

More than one teacher wrote on my report cards that I was too serious for a little boy and that I should laugh more. Yet, the awful truth was that I actually had a wicked sense of humor— even if my primary interest was to amuse myself and no one else. I also had a reputation I secretly enjoyed: if you tickled me, I absolutely would *not* laugh. I suppressed the normal reaction, offering up a deadpan, poker face in return. Or, in a staring contest, I would absolutely *not* be the first to blink. I was that competitive. However, I was just as fascinated with manipulating those I could exercise control over as I was with masking behavior others expected from a typical young boy. This was not a good combination of character traits. I once convinced my younger brother, Chris, to trust me and climb into a large black trunk, then locked it and slid it in a closet just to see how he would react. While I didn't keep him in there too long, it was long enough to traumatize him. In fact, I'm sure I gave him no indication I was planning to ever let him out. Just as I was unable to allow emotions to flow freely within myself, I also wasn't able to feel much for anyone else at the time.

* * *

The inability others had in suppressing their emotions truly fascinated me. I once played an elaborately executed prank on Chris, Angie, and Mark when our parents were not home. I acted out having eaten something that was poisonous and, slowly, over the course of nearly an hour, I pretended I was getting sicker and weaker and, finally, near death. Gagging and coughing and sinking to the floor, I urged them to call the poison control center, milking their natural responses in a scene of hopeless desperation. Near the end, I pretended I could only muster enough energy to give them the first six digits of a seven-digit phone number before I collapsed to the floor! First holding my breath and then breathing as shallowly as possible, I snapped my body as still as a corpse, shut my eyes, and listened. I had apparently given an Oscar-worthy performance; my brothers and sister were heaving with sobs. At that point, I popped up from the floor to show it was all a joke. But their emotions were so amped up, they could not simply hit the off switch like I had taught myself to do. Like *Star Trek's* Mr. Spock, I found their overflow of emotion to be...illogical. But, really, I had simply grown cold and manipulative. Having convinced myself I was born ugly, I had *become* ugly. I had learned not to like myself and I didn't really know how to care for other people. My center had gone dry. I had become an ingrown hair follicle, a hardened epithelial layer fit only to be peeled away and discarded.

I was stuck, weighed down with my childhood's end long before I had fully lived it. The loss of my smile, my laughter, my sense of connection with others—I was mired in more loss than I knew what to do with. Consequently, I slept just as heavily as I felt and for a couple of years into my early adolescence I still wet the bed from time to time. Remaining burrowed in my sleep was so much easier than rising up to face a new day. I was not afraid of the dark—because like some of the comic villains with fractured psyches I had spent much of my youth reading about, I too had grown up in the shadows. Since I had more control over my dreams than over reality, why not stay there? I certainly tried.

Nevertheless, during my waking hours I was willful enough to try to exercise control wherever I could, typically over my own emotions…or just my fears. Sometimes, when scaling the schoolyard walls to retrieve handballs knocked onto one of the lower roofs—a feat that most kids around the block wouldn't dare to try with so few light fixtures or window gates serving as handholds and toeholds to push off from—I would often pause before climbing back down to dangle my sneakers over the side of the rooftop parapet. I knew if I fell from such a height to the cement, I'd be seriously injured. I should have been more careful, but I had forgotten how. Taking risks like that made me feel in control, just like when I beat grown men playing handball or racquetball on the court—which I did more often than not as I grew to become a formidable player with extremely quick reflexes, sharp peripheral vision, and a long reach who could strike the ball with nearly equal accuracy with either my right or left hand. Years later as a young adult, I'd often acknowledge to friends that my drive to exercise control was so strong that I was probably well on my way to either becoming a reclusive and dangerous sociopath, or carefully planning my own suicide.

Then one day, unexpectedly, I bumped into God. It was just after my 12th birthday. Honestly, we Rollings were not a church-going family at all. As kids, we were taught to say prayers before going to bed like "Our Father, who art in Heaven, hallowed by thy name..." and "Now I lay me down to sleep, I pray the Lord my soul to keep; if I should die before I wake, I pray the Lord my soul to take." But that was the extent of it. It seemed like a good thing to do, but there was nothing heartfelt about the routine.

Everything changed one night as I was channel surfing. I happened upon a TV show called The PTL Club. A television preacher named Jim Bakker (who would later be disgraced for cheating on his wife and jailed for fraud) started talking about God's plan for my life. The simple message caught my attention. You see, I had *heard* of God but, in reality, God was just as distant to me as my own family. Yet, as I listened to Bakker, it struck me that *if* God had a plan for my life, it was worth finding out—since I didn't have a plan at all, and what I was doing clearly wasn't working. Even though I was young, I was already aware that the direction I was on wasn't going to end well for me. I didn't know where to start looking, but I was definitely ready to have a meeting with this God.

And, so, God found me where I was, sitting in front of a television set. It was a quick transaction. I asked Him to save me from myself, from the life I was barely living. I think, more than anything else at the time, I really appreciated God's attention to the messy details. Namely, me. For some time after our encounter, only He and I knew we had met. As typical, I didn't tell anyone my business. I started talking to God regularly. Not prayers, but conversations. Since Grandma was a member of St. Mark's Episcopal Church on Brooklyn Avenue, that's where I started attending. I was even confirmed there. But it was soon thereafter when the youth group was taken on a field trip to see an incredibly gory R-rated movie called "The Fury" (complete with exploding heads) that I stopped attending that particular church. Since I didn't know any other churches to attended, I started watching Christian television, ordering magazines such as *Discipleship Journal*, and listening to the award-winning "Unshackled" radio program produced by Pacific Garden Mission in Chicago. These regular half-hour dramatizations of the stories of others who had been found by God helped me to face myself and realize that I was not alone in having once been trapped.

my GOD?

although i am cut off from
You
and weak

too weak to reach
You

my God
please hear my whisper

i've heard You really love me
even though
well

You see the way i am

i finally know my need
but
well

i cannot find You

my God
You are infinity

i'm lost,
You see

can You find me please?

9

the human zoo

A drawing of an insane big cat, gifted to me by
one of my 3rd grade students.

WHILE I WAS ATTENDING Shell Bank Junior High School
in Sheepshead Bay, also known as Intermediate School 14
or I.S. 14, the school district determined that I should skip
seventh grade and my parents apparently agreed. Consistently outscoring classmates on reading and math grade level
assessments at the schools I attended, I don't recall that I was
given a choice. At the time, skipping a grade and getting
out of junior high school faster probably sounded like a
neat idea to me. In retrospect, moving any child out of his
or her schooling age group is an awful idea, especially for
one like me who was already a social misfit. Eighth grade,
like sixth grade before it, was pretty much a blur. On the

whole, I don't really remember much of anything about my middle school experience. Seriously. I don't remember any of my teachers. I don't remember walking the corridors of the building. I suspect the whole experience was either so traumatic or so inconsequential that I've blocked almost all of this particular chapter of my life from my memory. The few snippets and snapshots I can still recollect are all external to the school building itself. I remember the subway rides out to Sheepshead Bay as my train emerged gloriously from underground onto elevated platforms for the remainder of the trip, each car's dingy fluorescent lighting suddenly overwhelmed by sunlight. I remember the newspaper stand outside at the base of the staircase overshadowed by the elevated trestle, where I'd purchase several new Marvel comic books each week before getting on the bus.

I remember one particular cold day when—with my vision obscured by my parka hood fringed with fake fur and pulled tightly over my head—I stepped into a street intersection just a few blocks from school after getting off the bus I transferred to daily after the subway ride. Suddenly a car hood appeared before me and I was pinned in place— the car's tire had just parked itself on my foot as the driver slightly overshot his or her attempt to stop at the pedestrian crosswalk! The front of the car had missed hitting me by less than half an inch. I was told by the doctor that if the car had simply rolled all the way over my foot, it probably wouldn't have broken my toe—but because it came to rest all its weight directly on my foot, I ended up with a hairline fracture, the only broken bone I've ever had in my life. All my other memories of these middle school years were lost in the chemical admixture of adolescent trauma and hormones that must have been my life back then. However, I do have

convincing evidence that I completed all my requirements
and merited graduation from that missing experience in June
1976—a diploma tucked away in an aging orange album,
signed by my middle school principal, Milton J. Greenberg.
Oh, and I was also apparently good at math, based on my
Certificate of Award from the great Shell Bank Mathematics
Fair of May 1975.

I have a more vivid recollection of the drama over the
decision on where I was to go to high school. I had two
school guidance counselors attempting to persuade me, one
Black, one white. In my own heart, I wanted to take portfolio
exam to attend a specialized art high school in Manhattan.
The African American guidance counselor advised me to
make the safe, easy choice to stay within the same school
district and advance from Shell Bank to Sheepshead Bay
High School. It was the white guidance counselor who was
really listening to what I wanted to do and helped facilitate
a conversation with my parents about the appropriate next
steps. I remember being surprised at which of the counselors
supported my vision to pursue a career in the creative indus-
tries and which one didn't seem to read me at all. Or maybe
she felt that Black boys had it hard enough in the world as it
is without being caught up in a daydream.

*   *   *

Before I knew it, I had started as a student at the
High School of Art & Design on 57th Street in midtown
Manhattan. I was still only 12 years old. After school, I
rarely went straight home to Brooklyn. Instead, I went on
long self-guided walking excursions throughout New York
City, often walking dozens and dozens of blocks from the

East Side to the West Side, and uptown to downtown—
from novelty stores like Hammacher Schlemmer and FAO
Schwarz and their impossible-to-believe merchandise for
the rich, the famous, and the self-indulgent—to department
stores like Bloomingdales with its live cooking demonstra-
tions and expensive stuffed animals to purchase as gifts for
my friends—to the excesses of Times Square in its pre-family
friendly era when a glut of X-rated theaters still flaunted their
taboo—to the American Museum of Natural History with
its life-sized dioramas of biological life and the magnificent,
celestial shows cast onto the domed ceiling at Hayden Planetarium by its giant mechanical optical projector. I loved the
way the Planetarium's space shows induced me to recline all
the way back in my seat under a rotating blanket of projected
stars and just doze off without any penalty, as if I were safe in
my own private closet once again.

On one of my walks through the city, I made my first visit
to the Central Park Zoo just before it was renovated to elim-
inate the crueler, animal-injuring flaws in its original concrete
and iron bar design. But not before I saw something I've never
forgotten. That day, I watched as a large black panther, captured
from the wild, paced back and forth in a dark metal cage that
didn't seem any more than three times the animal's length from
nose to tip of tail. The silent, muscular cat was forced to pivot
quickly and sharply because its stride carried it across the cage
in a matter of seconds, leaving almost no maneuvering room
for its bulk. The cat's pacing never slowed. I watched for half
an hour and not once did the panther glance at any of us in the
gawking crowd. There was never a break in its pattern. Neither
the routine of his padded footfall nor the vacant glaze in his
eyes changed during the thirty minutes I spent staring at that
creature. I watched, horrified. And the longer I watched the

more certain I became that, before me, was a beautiful beast driven insane by the ugliness of its solitary confinement. I recognized myself in that caged, pacing animal. I longed for the creature to get out. And I wanted to escape, too.

*   *   *

By the time I became a student in EN 66 CRW-5, Ms. Waksman's 11th grade creative writing class, I already knew I loved stories. I didn't just read comics and watch movies—I immersed myself in them. Swimming in the stories that others had written about the lives that others live—whether those other lives were imagined or entirely true-to-life—allowed me the portals to escape my own story, even if only for an hour or two. It did not matter to me whether the stories were fiction or non-fiction—because I could enter in and comprehend them, they came to life as I rehearsed them over and again in my own mind. Through these reimaginings and remember-ings I discovered I had my own superpowers. Like one of Marvel's X-Men, I was born different. As I grew up, over time my difference developed into an advantage. I had mutated special abilities most human beings did not have to the degree that I possessed them. For example, I began to understand that my powers of observation were extraordinary. When I saw, I saw what most others overlooked. When I listened carefully, I was fully present. When I was daydreaming or just writing a poem, even if I was in your company I wasn't there at all. When I sang a familiar song or smelled a familiar smell, like the Nightcrawler, I could instantly transport myself to recollect thoughts and experiences that hadn't crossed my mind in years and had been forgotten. Like the bite by the radioactive spider that turned Peter Parker into Spiderman, my injury was the catalyst for the development of these unexpected abilities and more. I learned I could adapt observations into new ideas and models. I learned I could detect connections between things which on the surface were not at all alike and that would have otherwise remained apart. Like Doctor Manhattan in the DC Comics graphic novel series *Watchmen*, I learned that if I was injured I could repair myself, and that even if I was entirely annihilated I could simply reassemble and make myself whole again in another place and time—in another story. I learned I was a creator and that creation was an act of love, demanding my focus and investment in its process. I learned that I was patient with the process of loving for as long as it took for new life to appear as I made my art. And I learned my capacity to love and care for the needs of those I had attached to could sometimes be perceived as either overwhelming or inexplicable at best—coming from someone as difficult to read as I'd made myself to be.

For as long as I can remember, I've had vivid, technicolor dreams. Full participation dreams. My imagination is another one of my superpowers. In my dreams, for the most part I've always been the master of whatever worlds my imagination was able to create. There is however one recurring dream I've never been able to master—they are my Superman dreams. Well actually, my flying dreams. I didn't have a cape in these dreams, just a superpower. But the most significant thing about these dreams is how DIFFICULT it is for me to gain any sustained altitude above the sidewalk or streets. To defy gravity. In these dreams, I'm always physically exerting myself and entirely aware of the frustrating amount of effort I'm putting out; I often wake up sweating. It was in Ms. Waksman's class that I first experimented with

channeling my superpowers and abilities in another way—
writing stories that others could use to escape through. I also
began writing poetry in high school. Like my art at the time,
I wrote poetry in order to give it away, for the sole reason of
helping friends of mine who were down. I knew what it felt
like to suffer in silence, and when I saw someone else at risk
of being swallowed in the same kind of emotional abyss I had
barely escaped, I doubled back to help rescue them in the
only way I knew how. By investing my powers of observation
and patient focus into small acts of love.

I don't have any of the first generation of poems I ever
wrote back from when I started writing them in high school.
I'm sure they weren't very good. I used to write them up by
hand or type them at a typewriter or word processor, long
before I ever owned a computer that allowed me to save my
documents electronically. Still, I'm also sure they served their
purpose to those I gave them away to. What I do have is
my second generation of written poetry. I still wrote them
out by hand when I minored in creative writing as an undergraduate college student, but I'd learned by this time to save a
hard copy of everything I wrote in folders. Later on, I would
transcribe this second generation of writings on my first
desktop computer. Though each poem varies in its focus, the
following selections were all early tests of my power to create
a smile.

Honestly
(10/14/84)

There's this thing in my head that just needs to be said
Something I just <u>have</u> to tell you
You really and truly make me feel good
That's straight from the heart…
Honestly.

There is something about just my thinking of you
That brings a real smile to my face
'Cause you make me laugh (oh, you're <u>real</u> good at that!)
I appreciate you…
Honestly.

You must know that I love you—I'm sure that you do
(I've let you know often enough!)
But, you know, the best thing about being your friend is
I think you love me…
Honestly.

*   *   *

Not Quite a Love Poem
(5/6/85)

There's an unexpressed emotion I've begun to feel for you.
It's been getting sort of strong—I wasn't quite sure what to do
I've decided to express myself the best way I know how
So I'm writing you a poem and I wish to tell you now
That I think I need companionship—I think I'd prefer yours
I think I kind of like you more than any other girl
I think I'd treat you special in the way that you deserve
And I know that you inspire me to think up pretty words
For I think you have the brightest I that I have ever seen
They're symbolic of your character if you know what I mean
You see, I see you as a bird in flight in all you say and do
It's the sweetness of your soul that keeps attracting me to you
Now honestly, I don't quite know how strong you feel for me
I don't want to come on heavy—but I do want you to see
That you make it really easy for a guy to fall in love
And if you should ever fall for me…I thank my Lord above

That's all I really have to say—I hope I've said it well
And if we're meant to be together only time will tell
This isn't quite a love poem—it's just my way to say
If I could share my life with you, I'd see no better way.

*   *   *

Butterfly Song
(May 1985)

Butterflies fly, so why can't I?
Oh, why can't I take flight?!
I want to sprout little butterfly wings
and flutter out of sight.

I'd ride the breezes of the air—
I'd soar across the skies
and bounce up and down in a butterfly dance
to everyone's surprise.

I want to be a little butterfly—
Oh, don't think that this is odd!
'Cause a butterfly's life rests securely in
the mighty hands of God.

*   *   *

The next few poems are strictly exercises in my powers of observation, either distilling a memory down to its essence, or boiling down something happening in front of my eyes until I've removed all of the words that are unnecessary in order to convey the story.

The Addict
(Fall 1985)

A young man with an old face
dirt in its cracks and filth on his clothing
    struggles to keep from slowly
      sinking as he tries to remain
      standing on the corner of a sidewalk
unable to notice
the vehicles that pass him by
or the people that ignore him.

*   *   *

The Subway Station
(Fall 1985)

a concrete platform crowded with people
shifting impatiently
along its edges
waiting
in oppressive air
for the light at the end of the tunnel.

*   *   *

Untitled Journal Entry
(written on the island of Jamaica)
(7/2/87)

Barefoot in my yellow room
with nobody else
but God and my pen…
looking for words to write.

*   *   *

In these final three poems selected from dozens I have written, I sought only to express the emotion that had always eluded me the most in life—until I realized I had the power to create the love I needed within me all along.

Early Winter
(Spring 1986)

The smooth moon slithers
through the shutters
of my northwest window;
elusive on this cloudy night,
its face plays hide and seek;
through the vapors of the frigid sky
forming crystal droplets on my window pane
this early winter spent without you.

*   *   *

mid-morning sea gust
(c. 1987)

Seagulls are calling above my shoulder. I sit at the far edge of the ocean. A gust as wide as this stretch of beach floods in from the curved horizon to rip past my ears, possessing the bodies of the quivering birds, tussling the virgin white tips of their feathers. The unruly flock swings in urgent rhythm with currents that first circled the earth and now stir the ocean. Rippling and diving, pausing and calling, the birds ride incessant morning winds.

An iridescent piece of shell is tossed ashore in a briny splash; it slips into the nearby sand, set free from the heavy pulse of the sea.

I flinch from the light that strikes my eyes, reflecting off the wet shell's back. Ocean foam bubbles over my toes and splashes around my bare thighs, rocking the shard as each new sheet is drawn back. I reach for the shell and stroke her glistening skin. I stare at the sky with a wide open face. I smile at the smack of the next gust of air. The silver fragment tumbles dryly from my careless hands.

Seagull calls are in my ears, the music of lonely lovers. A cold hard wave crashes the beach and steals the precious shell away. The water's salt stings my eyes. I draw my knees to my face. I wrap my arms around my legs.

I close my eyes tight. I hear your name in the roar. Sunlight warms the back of my neck.

*   *   *

moment romance
(c. 1987)

Caught in the warmth of a lady's arms
hands of calm stroking cool my face
and knowing that I'm quite alright
for this one breezy, unexpected night
soaked in New York City lights
drinking bold and watery eyes
rippling with delight
in the comfort of my sight

I hold her
and romance her
as this moment flickers on
as two live wires spark and ignite
burning bright in our private night

Resisting

the parting the dawning will bring
as we two fall away
to separate yards
and ashen days
in remembrance of what might have been...

I stare into eyes that are no longer there
were you ever really here?

I sigh
the moment disappears

maybe once again next year.

*   *   *

Through my poetry and storytelling, through my super-powers, I discovered I could write myself free of the human zoo that still held me captive, offering up my observations of the full menagerie that constitutes our shared existence. I could retell the stories we live by. I could stop time and turn it backwards. I could teleport myself to safe places. I could rescue my friends from the threatening abyss. I could bring the dead back to life.

Diary Entry

The days move
as slowly as they wish;

the heat licks around my head
coating skin in perspiration;

the mosquitoes will sting me as i sleep
yet i am helpless to stop them.

10

college trials & tribulations

A pencil self-portrait drawn during
my years at The Cooper Union.

WHEN I BEGAN HIGH school in September of 1976, I got
to sample various studio art and graphic design rotations
through 9th and 10th grades. It was during the two months
of one of my rotational art classes in my sophomore year
that I had my first and only Black male teacher in all of my
schooling from first through twelfth grade. His name was
Mr. Graves. I remember nothing else about him but his last
name, his moustache with its waxed and twisted ends, and

his salt-and-pepper goatee beard. Ultimately, I decided to major in architecture during my junior and senior years of high school. I learned the fundamentals of drafting, interior design, and modelmaking, but mostly I remained interested in the buried complexity beneath obvious appearances. I selected the following pen and ink drawing for my page in my high school senior yearbook, part of an underground complex I had mapped out.

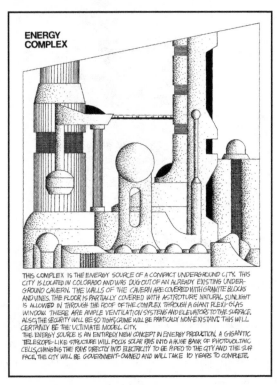

A drawing I submitted for my 1980 high school
graduation yearbook.

Like this one, the structures I conceived were often partially buried into the banks of steeply graded hills and fortified with fieldstone retaining walls. I liked shelters that were bunkered and hard to discern from their natural surroundings. I lived on the Honor Roll throughout high school. I won Honor Roll certificates for excellence in science, mathematics, and social studies in ninth grade. I won Honor Roll certificates for excellence in overall scholarship in January and June of 1977, again in January and June of 1978, and again in June of 1979 when I was also elected as a member of the New York City chapter of the National Honor Society of Secondary Schools. I ultimately graduated from the High School of Art & Design in 1980, earning a Diploma with Honors, along with awards in Architecture, English, Writing, and Biology. And yet it felt like I left as quietly as I'd arrived. I was one of four students from my high school graduating class who had successfully passed the entrance examination to the vaunted Cooper Union School of Architecture. I began college in September of that same year when I was still 16 years old. My first year, working under gentle old walrus-mustached Professor Chester (Chet) Wisniewski was so much like Mr. Gupta's architecture class at Art & Design I flew through it with A's. In my second year, I was receiving C's in my Architecture major. By my third year, I was given an F in my architectural studio section. I was absolutely stunned. I had never failed a class before. I was sometimes in courses with students who were returning to college for the second time to change their careers. So, as the youngest person in my freshman class, I typically remained invisible to most of my peers, well outside of their social circles and alone in my struggles.

*　　*　　*

Grandma died in 1980 and as a consequence I developed my first deeply held prejudice. While it's proper to note her passing given how deeply I felt about her, I'm typically blunt in my assessment of the circumstances that led to her death and it's also appropriate that I convey that truth in this writing. To my mind on the day of Grandma's death, and to my mind even to this day, it's more accurate to say that Grandma was killed. Not by an act of malice. EVERYONE loved Grandma. No, it was negligence that killed my grandmother. In the weeks prior to the day of her death, Grandma had a serious accident in the kitchen where she was cooking when she accidentally laid her hand on a burner with an open flame. As senior citizens age, they often develop a reduced sensitivity to pain because of decreased blood flow to their nerve endings. This is how Grandma originally ended up in the hospital; she had acquired a severe burn on her hand before she was able to recognize that her flesh was being injured. Grandma's hand almost immediately ballooned and in the hospital the doctors even had to cut the wedding band from her hand to save her dangerously swollen finger as the circulation was cut off.

But this was only an unforeseeable accident. No one was at fault at this point and the burn to her hand isn't what killed my grandmother. Here's what did. While she was in the hospital, Grandma spent time in the Intensive Care Unit (ICU) where her respiration was supported with oxygen for a period of time. So this frail and beautiful woman with a severe case of asthma was bought home from an oxygen-rich environment to her own bed—lovingly welcomed and watched over by several of my relatives who were either smoking in her vicinity or simply carrying invisible layers of second-hand smoke allergens in and out of her bedroom. I was not at home yet from school that day but I know from personal experience

how this went. I have never yet encountered a smoker who
fully understands the effect of their lighting up and circulating about the same house as a person with asthma. They
might excuse their cigarette or even try to exhale smoke out
of the corners of their mouths rather than directly in your
face, but the one thing they never seem think to do is to avoid
lighting up a cigarette at all.

The triggers for an allergy-induced asthma attack are like
a cascade effect; the body's sensitivity to allergens or invading
particles increases with each successive exposure, escalating the
effort to protect itself until it reaches a tipping point and a
point of no return. The airways swell and constrict, overpro-
ducing protective mucous, as the muscles that work to draw in
breaths tighten and strain to do their natural work. And that's
how Grandma was killed. Grandma did not die of natural
causes. She was brought home from the hospital to her jubilant
family—full of smokers coming in and out of her bedroom.
Grandma was quiet, like me. I'm sure she was conflicted as
she was surrounded by her dear children and grandchildren. I
doubt that my grandmother was very vocal about the matter
of her increasing difficulty at drawing a breath, but if so, it was
only after it was too late. Right there in the comfort of her own
bed, Grandma had an asthma attack on the night she came
home from the hospital after days spent in the ICU. And as a
result of that asthma attack on the night she came home from
the hospital, my grandmother subsequently dropped dead
from a heart attack right there beside her own bed.

When I arrived home, there was an ambulance outside of
1258 Lincoln Place. Slowly, the story of what had happened
was relayed to me. And my immediate response was a quiet
seething anger at the pure stupidity of every smoker that
wafted their second-hand debris into the airspace of Grandma

that evening. One of my older cousins kept bawling about
how many people it took to lift the dead weight of Grandma's
collapsed body back into the bed. Still seared in my memory
is the picture of my Uncle Eddie sobbing into the crook of
his arm, face against the wall, as he stood beside the bed
where his mother had just died. Uncle Eddie is the one who
had brought Grandma home and it was clear that he felt the
deepest guilt even though he wasn't a smoker himself.

It was on that night that I developed a prejudice against
all smokers everywhere, all at once. I love my cousins, but this
prejudice has never left me. And I'll never be able to breathe
freely around a smoker.

*   *   *

I was once with a group of undergraduate classmates on
a lithography class excursion to the Museum of Modern Art
(called the MoMA for short) to see a special collection of
prints on a day when the museum was closed to the public.
We entered glass doors to the grand lobby and lined up at the
large reception desk. Having started college so very young,
I was still rather self-absorbed. So, I was not really paying
attention to what our course instructor was doing at the head
of the line as she facilitated our entry into the museum. Never
talkative or chatty, I was simply observing my surroundings
with great curiosity since I rarely visited museums.

I stood in the midst of my classmates and their hushed
conversations, dressed in faded jeans and old sneakers just as
most of them were. As usual, I wore a black backpack with
all my belongings, keeping my hands free. As the line was
making its way past the reception desk, a security guard called
my attention. I gave it to him casually. He asked if he could

help me. I shook my head slowly, trying to decipher what felt at that moment to be a strangely coded message. The guard clarified that the delivery entrance was on the side of the building, implying I was in the wrong place. Suggesting I was a messenger rather than a member of the group in front of him. I felt like I had been slapped upside my head with his powerful, uniform-clad words, sucker-punched by a representative of the MoMA, the institution on whose property I stood. I was left stinging. Embarrassed at being singled out, at first I wondered if anyone else had heard his comment. None of my classmates seemed to react at all. Nor were any of my classmates approached in this fashion. I was alone in our little crowd. It was then that I noticed what the guard must have seen, that I was the only African American in the group. Frankly, I had never given real thought before as to how this must have appeared since it was a visual dynamic I could not gaze upon while occupying my own body. The silence of my counterparts while I fought back a growing fury only served to reinforce our differences. They were clueless— entirely unaware of the gravity of the story happening right in front of them. They were white and weightless.

I responded with great effort to control my breathing, to contain my response, to cap my rising emotion, and not embarrass myself further by causing a scene. I focused on the guard alone, telling him that I was a student, a part of the group in front of him just like everyone else there. I wanted him to tell me why he thought I was *different* from everyone else. I wanted him to expose his own prejudice. He did not cooperate. Nevertheless, I knew the answer before I asked him. I already knew, deep down I knew. I was a Black, male college student in the early 1980s. Was I that rare? The guard I was addressing was also Black. Yet he looked at me like I was speaking to him in an alien tongue emerging from an alien body in alien circumstances. He didn't seem to understand that all I wanted was a declaration of his guilt. He didn't offer one. I was trapped between my desire to bodily pursue him and vocally force a response, and my desire to keep my cool, hidden in the background. I could not do both. The guard never answered me. I choked down the unspent emotion as we entered the elevator. No one spoke to me. My lips were pressed together hard, my eyebrows squeezed into stiff furrows and my eyes did not attempt to meet anyone else's.

Head down, burdened beneath my own bedeviled thoughts, I did not notice as we approached a second reception desk on the upper floor that housed the special collection. As I was about to step past, I mistakenly met the eyes of a blond-haired young lady with a bright smile and a sharp suit mouthing out loud the same question aimed at me moments before, "May I *help* you?" My response was loud this time, piercing the museum's quiet: "No, you may not help me! I am with the group!"

I now had everyone's attention whether I wanted it or not. I think my course instructor may have spoken up at this point to say we were all together but I cannot remember that really, any more than I can remember anything about the special collection I went to see that day. The next thing I remember with vivid clarity was the walk from the museum to the subway. I had peeled away from the group because all I felt was my skin. I felt my skin tingling as though it were not truly a part of my body. I felt all of its surfaces amazingly, shockingly apparent. I had been stripped naked against my will. I was exposed. My skin was radiating messages, heating my blood, glowing brightly with colors, marking my escape, calling me out, hotter underneath its flesh than the sun on the surface of it on that particularly humid day. I had never felt my skin weighing upon my thin frame before. I felt like I was wearing skin, as if it were covering me like heavy, perspiration-soaked drapes flung over my head, making me appear to all passersby as if I were just a messenger. A mere messenger to be given directions and sent quickly on his way in and out of side entrances. I was a first-generation college student on a full tuition scholarship at the Cooper Union but no one walking past me could see that. My skin was all in the way. Fully aware of myself as others saw me, I felt ashamed and angry at what I was wearing—not the torn jeans and beat-up sneakers, but the skin.

*   *   *

In my fourth year at the Cooper Union School of Architecture, I was forced to repeat third-year architectural design. Professor Anthony Candido became my head professor. He was one of three or so full professors in the department whose opinion of your work was life or death at final critiques. Adjuncts, even if they advised and supported your project throughout the semester, did not dare dissent with the lead architecture professors at those critiques. The hierarchy was traditionally ingrained and absolutely unwavering. One of my friends who also graduated from the High School of Art & Design and was accepted into the Cooper Union, a tall blond fellow named John, was totally shredded at an end-of-the-semester critique the previous year—Professor Raimund Abraham, an Austrian gentleman, stood up at this public forum to which the whole architecture school was invited and actually took a pencil to sketch what he argued were better solutions across the surface of the careful final renderings John had pinned up on the white walls. John did not return to Cooper Union the following academic year. In fact, statistics at the time showed that only 55% of those accepted into the School of Architecture completed the five-year undergraduate program.

When, in the first weeks of my fourth year of study, Professor Candido candidly stated to me that while my attitude was fine he doubted my aptitude, I knew the department had made up its mind; I struggled daily and to no avail beneath the weight of its decision for the rest of the academic year. It was a kind of existential torture. I didn't want to be there, but I had to be there, but being there every day was never going to change the outcome of my final year majoring in architecture at an institution founded for students like me by Peter Cooper, the self-taught American industrialist and philanthropist. Professor Rod Knox, a light-skinned Black professor who I never saw without a bow tie, pulled me aside to whisper one day that I would have been better off if I had gone to a school like Pratt Institute in Brooklyn. What he chose not to elaborate was that Pratt was considered by high-minded Cooper Union professors at that time to possess a lesser caliber architecture program aimed at preparing more conventional students. That might have been one of the two or three times that Professor Knox ever spoke to me. He was pleasant. And I was a dead man walking.

During that final year I did all I could to hide my shame. Just to hide, actually. I won't say what I did with my nights to escape. During the days I spent studio time in perpetual embarrassment, evading faculty, disassociating from peers, finding unlocked, unused storage rooms in the Foundation Building of the Cooper Union in which I could sit in the dark and pray and cry. I would do so for hours at a time. Those rooms befriended me, closed in on me, protected me. I was never interrupted. I almost lost my mind. The pain was palpable and always just beneath the surface. And at the end of that academic year,

I received yet another F and an academic dismissal by chain-smoking Associate Dean Richard Henderson. I was forced to leave the school. Not knowing what was ahead, I picked up where I had left off with my summer employment and began a stint as a free-lance architectural modelmaker. In my state of personal ruin, I found in the artistry and craft of modelmaking a map for another kind of college identity. In 1985, I became a "transfer" student into The Cooper Union School of Art. I flourished. I took two semesters in a row of calligraphy instructed by a brilliant professor named Donald Kunz. I also took two semesters in a row of creative writing instructed by an equally brilliant professor named Brian Swann. I took three semesters each of photography, printmaking, and advanced drawing. I won awards again. I made discoveries. I found color to be more of a friend than the shadows in the hidden nooks and crannies throughout the Cooper Union's landmark Foundation Building.

During my creative renaissance, I also found my voice for social justice. The presence of African Americans throughout the Cooper Union faculty and student body had long been underrepresented. Underrepresentation had consequences inside my school building similar to those outside what should have been a safe space for learning for me. Once, I walked into an office in a suite on the second floor of the Foundation Building to say hello to one of my friends working behind a secretary's desk for her work-study assignment. As we began to exchange greetings and small talk, a woman on staff in that same office stepped out into reception area from a back room where she had been working with the sunny greeting of, "Hi, do you have something for me?" I'm sure I looked confused, so she followed with the question, "You are the messenger, aren't you?" Thunder clouds quickly formed over my head. I chose not to yell in her face that I was a Cooper Union student. Instead, I turned my back on her and shouted out this fact as I stormed out of the office door.

I wanted to contribute to an environment of activism calling out the ease and frequency of such slights and oversights as they were faced by students like me. I wanted to do my part to help overcome the general apathy of both the Cooper Union administration and the majority of its white students toward addressing the problems of underrepresentation head on. I was elected as President of ONYX, the Black Student Society at Cooper Union and began to work directly with the Dean of Students, Marilyn Gore, and Marina Gutierrez, the longtime Director of the Cooper Union's Saturday Art & Architecture Program, on ways to increase the visibility of the persons of color in our institution. I gathered demographic statistics and examined Cooper Union's bylaws and Board of Trustee mandate to promote the high-quality tuition-free college education it had historically provided and make it accessible to those who could most benefit economically from it, while also making the population of Cooper Union more accurately reflect the diverse population of New York City. I then wrote an open letter to our school newspaper *The Cooper Pioneer*, describing the problem at hand to all of our faculty, students, and administrative staff. I immediately followed up that letter with a proposal I drafted to outline some possible solutions. My school followed through on one of the points I proposed by establishing a new Committee for the Enhancement of a Minority Presence at the Cooper Union.

By the time I arrived at my senior year as an undergraduate Art major in 1988, I wanted to mount a one-man show with artwork that spoke out loud about the injustices I had experienced in the School of Architecture…yet overcoming anyway. Initially, I wasn't sure I had enough artwork to fill the Sixth Floor Gallery so I went into overdrive making new art to accomplish my goal. I titled my senior exhibition "40 Works of Art after Liberation from the Cooper Union School of Architecture, or, One Black Student's Point of View." I used a combination of portraits, prints, and photographs to fill the space and hung it with the help of my dear friend Hope Blake, a sister from Jamaica who also attended the School of Art. I wrote a manifesto and painted it floor to ceiling on one of the walls on why I had given my show this title. Then I invited all of my old Architecture professors. All of them. I still possess a sign-in book filled with affirming comments by many who attended the opening of my show. And, as the first college graduate in the Rolling family, I was honored to win the Cooper Union Alumni Association Award for Service to the School. This period of my life was also documented in a two-page article I was interviewed for, one of a series of student profiles published in the 1988-89 Cooper Union Annual Report.

Sitting alongside my award-winning color pencil
and oil pastel portrait titled *Gemstone.*

So, after three years of being unable to step onto the third floor of the Foundation Building where all the architecture studios were located without my heart beating up into my throat and breaking out into a sweat, I was finally able to stuff my trauma and shame into a memorial sarcophagus of my own making as I pinned up the fliers advertising my exhibition on all the bulletin boards throughout the school. I could now present 40 pieces of evidence that I was more than they thought I was.

*   *   *

Clark was different than me. He had learned to be an artist's artist, with a visual orientation through and through. Clark was a sculptor. Large-scale, exquisitely crafted, highly polished wooden assemblies. Like me, Clark was also in the Master of Fine Arts (M.F.A.) graduate program at Syracuse University. His devotion to working in his studio and the woodshop stood out as he spent his days and nights in the arts facilities. He was awarded a teaching assistantship to support his studies and only a year after his graduation, Clark had parlayed his intensity of focus—and, I must add, his privilege as a white, male art major—into an adjunct university faculty position teaching first-year sculpture. That kind of trajectory, straight from college student to college professor, wasn't even conceivable for a Black, first-generation college student like myself at the time. It isn't any more likely a career path even now, some thirty years later.

I now confess to the deep sense of inadequacy I held at the time when comparing myself with Clark. Even though I had identified as an artist since I was a child, was I the artist that Clark was? I asked myself this question numerous times. But because I could not convince myself to devote the entirety of my time as a visual arts major to living, cooking, and sleeping on a futon in the small graduate art studio I was provided, I also could not reconcile my identity as an artist with the pristine and widely applauded example that Clark never failed to present. Moreover, none of the art faculty took me aside to show me the ropes and simply tell me what was expected of me as a graduate student. As usual, I was on my own.

I had been accepted into the M.F.A. graduate studies program in Printmaking and Drawing in the College of Visual & Performing Arts (VPA) at Syracuse University in 1988, upon earning a full-tuition fellowship in the university's African American Studies department. How I ended up being awarded a full fellowship is a story in itself. I had applied to only two universities—Syracuse University and the University of Michigan as I recall—the only two I met the qualifications for which offered full fellowships in African American Studies with an annual stipend to pay for living expenses. I simply could not afford to continue my higher education otherwise. Still, I did not ask my parents to pay a cent to help me. They had three other children to get through college. While I had sent my application in on time, it sat on someone's desk past the deadline. I was told after the fact by an administrator in that office that my application was found under a pile well after the deadline even though there was still more funding remaining to be awarded. When my application was unburied and came to light, the administrator quickly concluded that I was more than qualified for a full ride so she erased the dates on the paperwork and made it appear to the university like my application was submitted well in advance.

In my first year as a VPA student, the studio faculty in Printmaking and Drawing quickly realized that given my eclectic background and interests—which ranged from having been an undergraduate architecture major and a free-lance architectural modelmaker, to having studied drawing, printmaking, photography, calligraphy, and creative writing with equal passion—I was more ideally suited to complete my degree as a major in Studio Research.

For this reason, I transferred over to what would turn out to be one of the last cohorts of students to graduate from the Studio Research program. Studio Research was one of a group of degree programs that constituted the college's Experimental Studios department. Originally formed in 1970, Experimental Studios was ultimately dismantled at the start of the 1990s because the university would no longer commit to marketing its unique interdisciplinarity to attract new students. The Experimental Studios department was founded and advised by about seven very diverse faculty members who came from all over the spectrum of the college's studio art and design disciplines, yet shared a common creative vision for maintaining a program that was open-ended enough to allow, for example, an industrial design student who really loved sculpture to shape a path of coursework to fit their own needs and interests without being confined to a rigid set of program requirements and expectations. While every student was required to take a core course that incorporated all of the different represented disciplines, every student was also allowed various opportunities to "think outside the box," a propensity that stays with me to this day.

In keeping with this freedom to journey back and forth over creative boundaries, it was unnatural to spend 100% of my time thinking only about visual ideas. Once again, I was not Clark. Instead, a third of my time was spent either researching in the African American Studies department library or at my off-campus apartment writing poetry. Another third of my time was spent in service—either as the president of Newbirth Fellowship in Christ, a campus student organization, as editor-in-chief of the Black Voice Magazine, or as an officer or informal advisor in a couple of the other African American student associations. Consequently, Clark produced a lot more works of visual art than I did. I tried to compensate for my guilt and my perpetual sense of falling short of expectations by requesting that my studio professors also consider the effort and artistry I put into my non-visual experiments as part of their final grading evaluations each semester. Fortunately, they complied.

Because I had minored in creative writing at the Cooper Union during my undergraduate B.F.A. studies in the School of Art, and also because I was doing LOTS of writing as a Fellow in the African American Studies department during my years at Syracuse University, I felt comfortable electing to write a Master's thesis rather than choosing to mount a thesis exhibition. I had a body of visual work, but I also had a body of writing and my choice was supported. My thesis committee included Donald Lee DuSell, Professor of Studio Research and my advisor; David MacDonald, Professor of Ceramics and the only African American tenured full professor in the School of Art prior to my achievement of the same rank many years later; Bruce Manwaring, Professor of Print-making; Jerome Malinowski, Professor of Studio Research; and Dr. Randolph Hawkins, Chair of the African American Studies department and also the chair of my Master's thesis examining committee. My initial thesis draft was about 80 pages long, an exploration of American visual culture, spirituality, and personal identity. However, my thesis examining committee didn't think it was rigorous enough! So

my committee made me write it over again from scratch, a
process that would take another year of research and word
craft. This is how my 2-year M.F.A. degree program stretched
to become a three-year journey and why I am a 1991 Syracuse
University graduate, and not a 1990 graduate as originally
planned. I completed my thesis revisions while living out of
the basement at 1260 Lincoln Place, which my family and
I converted into an unfinished apartment to accommodate
my unexpected return home from college after two years of
living on my own. My final thesis turned out to be about
120 pages long, titled "Ultimately other Than WEST: The
Promise of Jesus Christ and Artistry in His Name," successfully presented and unanimously approved on April 8, 1991.

I would spend the next year courting and preparing to
marry Me'Shae La'Suel Brooks, a young woman from the
small city of Anderson, Indiana whom I met as she was
completing her Master of Public Administration degree
on a full fellowship from the vaunted Maxwell School at
Syracuse University. As the first boyfriend she'd ever had,
after proposing to Me'Shae, I travelled to the Midwest for the
first time to ask her very strict and skeptical parents for her
hand in marriage. Even though they consented, it was also
abundantly clear that they did not fully trust a New Yorker.
Me'Shae and I were married on August 1, 1992. And thus
commenced the most difficult trial I would face up to that
date: creating a viable career path from higher education to
my higher purpose. Whatever that was.

Return Visit

they
disregarded my presence
violated my faith
cut my supply
left me to die

never turned toward my work table again
wasted me
left me to die

somehow
I'm still alive

sometimes
a new home is found
in the unlikeliest of places.

on the site of engineered calamity
of carefully administered abandonment
the strange chalky odor
of demolished architecture
suspended in mists heavy
above the floorboards of my ruin
I found shelter
from hard ink nights
from the threat of degrading measurements
collapsing perspective
and uneven lines

within charcoal constructions
softly contoured by my hand
supported firmly
on white sheets of paper

and the human figure held me safe

11

stuck in the basement

Working with my students as a New York City
elementary school art teacher.

I NEVER ACTUALLY PLANNED to become a teacher. I just
stumbled into the calling. Teaching is a *giving* profession, but
I had learned very little about being a giver as I was growing
up. In my personal life at that time of my life outside of
school, I was still learning how to be a friend to others and,
also, how easy it is to hurt those you want to love and support
if you're not truly paying attention. How did I learn to give?

As I exited my teen years and entered young adulthood,
I began to push beyond my familiar limits in the effort to
connect meaningfully with others. I worked to show myself

friendly. I wanted to build relationships, reaching out to others rather than waiting for other people to reach out to me. I made LOTS of mistakes, but along the way I also learned to pay very careful attention to what other people were communicating in both their words and their silent cues. My progress was slow. I remember Salimah; I tried way too hard to be her *best* friend, crowded her, and drove her away. I remember my high school crush on Carola Zakura Rosas Kawamoto—half Japanese, half Peruvian—long after we had graduated. But my feelings for her were obscured by our friendship and I could never figure out how to mean more to her. I remember becoming so close with my friends Peppy and Sharon from Beulah Church of the Nazarene, we became a sort of "Three Musketeers" and did everything with each other in mind for years.

In my early teens after I had left St. Mark's Episcopal Church, I ended up at the Beulah Church of the Nazarene for several years, which happened to be on Troy Avenue and St. John's Place right around on the corner from where I lived. I became one of the lead singers in Beulah's gospel band, a difficult choice for me because of my extreme shyness. No songs I led never sounded the way they did at rehearsals because all the muscles in my throat would constrict from the anxiety of the moment, cutting off the air I needed to support each note. Nevertheless, I kept singing. Opening my mouth in vocal worship also opened me up to God like nothing else. Beulah was the first church I ever attended where there were other young people who sought after the Lord like I did. Openly. Willing to lay our emotions out on the table. I still sang because it made me cry and I knew I *needed* to cry. I needed to cry because I realized that the release of my own toxic emotions was an invitation for God to come fill with his overflow what I'd just emptied out through song. Without fail, the Holy Spirit entered every time I opened up and let Him come in and each time I was filled with a much-needed inrush of health and vitality. Some of us would sneak over to the Brooklyn Tabernacle on Flatbush Avenue to visit its Tuesday night prayer meetings or its Sunday services. I say "sneak" because some of the leadership at Beulah were vocal about not understanding why we couldn't find everything we needed at Beulah.

I remember my brief friendship with Yvonne which turned into an even briefer flash-in-the-pan romance that quickly burned out; as a consequence I developed a mantra I still use today, that "I am a former perfectionist who doesn't try quite so hard anymore."

I remember Jacqui, my brief fiancée's younger sister, and how I sensed right from the start that what she needed most from me was to help her feel safe and protected. Over 30 years later, Jacqui still pushes me today to make myself more visible, even in this writing.

Most of all, I remember the deepening desire to give. Growing up ugly meant that the very same habits that kept me safe as a child were stunting my development into a healthy adult. I struggled to enter a new plane of productive relationships.

*   *   *

My high school was a huge fixture in the Rolling household. While I had graduated from the High School of Art & Design in 1980, my younger brother Dwayne would graduate in 1983 three years after me and works today as a professional graphic designer in North Carolina. But long before me, my father had *also* graduated from this very same high school in 1956, back when it was still called the School of Industrial Art! There is a myth that those who can, make art, and those who can't, teach art. I know this to be a myth, because when I transferred to become an undergraduate Cooper Union School of Art student and agreed to teach 3D Design and Sculpture over two consecutive years to 11th and 12th grade high school students attending the Cooper Union's Saturday Art & Architecture Program, I already knew I could make art. I had grown up making it, as the son of a professional artist. I knew what the *aha!* moment felt like intimately. And yet, from 1986 to 1988, I was never more moved than when I saw that *aha!* moment reflected in the eyes and the ideas of my first students over and over and over again. Those years as a Saturday Program instructor under the guidance of Marina Gutierrez mark the earliest point at which I began to understand that it wasn't enough for me to be an artist—alone in my studio figuring out what to do next. I was compelled to think about what it might mean to become an arts educator, a creative catalyst in the midst of the mess of creative identities exploding into existence. I wanted to help shape human potential. I wanted to be a creativity teacher.

It wasn't until I had finished my second college degree at Syracuse University where I was still focused on developing my personal visual arts and creative writing practices, that I realized I wanted to give my best habits away to kids who were walking a similar path. Kids who were misfits like me. I wanted to teach art and design. Basically, I wanted to teach creativity—acts of generosity I consider to be one of the highest forms of giving. But no one was hiring and my résumé wasn't selling me. I was newly married to my wife Me'Shae. Yet as we began our first year as a married couple, I was still without a steady income. Even with a master's degree in my dresser drawer, I could not find a decent-paying job. One place, the Christian High School of Staten Island, was ready to hire me on three separate occasions and each time, for different reasons, the opportunity fell through. I was generally depressed that I could not find a way to get started at giving my best away.

While I would eventually go on to earn two more college degrees, both in arts education, at that point in my fledgling and sputtering career, I had never once taken a college course preparing me to be a teacher. But I had gathered some experience along the way working with teenagers and young adults as a Sunday School teacher, as a counselor to runaways and homeless youth at Covenant House, and as an hourly wage art instructor in New York City public schools. So, I naturally figured I was most suited to work with older kids. A friend named Barrington from my home church at that time, the Brooklyn Tabernacle, had decided not to accept a part-time job offer teaching after school at Hunter College Elementary School (HCES) and suggested that I should interview for the position instead. But I was so discouraged after over a year of unemployment and under-employment that I had absolutely no confidence I was qualified to work with young children. Would kids even have any fun at all learning in my classroom? Believe it or not, the extended-day program director who hired me, Marcella Lemonnier, actually had to *convince* me to take the job when she made the offer!

The year was 1993. I'd just been hired to teach art and creative writing after school in the basement level of a school building for gifted learners that strangely had almost no windows. Likewise, I still had no unobstructed sight-lines to my immediate future. This was just a part-time job, paying $10 an hour but with no medical or other benefits. And no matter how hard I tried, I could not see any way out of that basement with its low-hung ceilings just inches above my head. After my first year at HCES, I struggled to find a better job elsewhere over the summer but failed. So, I went back to Hunter the following Fall, more frustrated than ever that I could not do any better given all the years I had put into pursuing a higher education. This pattern of disappointment—giving my best to my students, earning very little money, seeking a better paying job, failing to do so, and returning to Hunter—repeated itself for most of the remainder of that decade. It really seemed like I was going nowhere. Yet, I was so tangled up at the center of the pattern, I could not see how the contours of my world at the basement level were slowly evolving from year to year.

For example, in my second year at what was called the "Hunter Clubhouse" extended-day program, I applied for an additional job as a substitute teacher, working upstairs during the regular school day. For that entire year, absolutely no one called upon me to substitute in his or her classroom. No one. The next year, I was called upstairs to substitute 24 times, for grade levels ranging from kindergarten to fifth grade. The year after that, I was called to substitute over 60 times! And yet, I *still* tried to exit the basement of HCES each summer in search of a better paying job. In 1996, I was hired full-time as an assistant teacher at Hunter College Elementary School for a combined classroom of first- and second-graders, while continuing to work as a part-time instructor for "Hunter Clubhouse" after the regular school day had ended. By this time, the director of the extended-day program was Ms. Patricia Lambert, a beloved and veteran early childhood educator who subsequently became the elementary school's principal.

Patricia served as an important early mentor to me and provided unfailing encouragement when I made the difficult decision to return to college in 1995 for a second master's degree, this time in the field of education. Patricia was also kind enough to write one of my reference letters during the admissions application process. By 1997, I was offered a position as director of the "Hunter Clubhouse" program to which I was first hired so reluctantly.

Moving from confusion to confidence, uncertainty to clarity, and from failure to success required some major shifts in how I was processing the day-to-day experiences that were weighing me down. First, I began focusing on what I was presently able give to others much more than on what I did not have or had not yet achieved. There is a verse in the Bible that says: "Do nothing from selfish ambition or conceit, but in humility count others more significant than yourselves." Notice it doesn't say not to have ambition; on the contrary, we can have as much ambition as we'd like, as long as it isn't entirely self-centered. At Hunter College Elementary School, I became ambitious about teaching. In fact, my competitiveness was genuinely provoked by encountering so many new teachers younger than I was, teachers with only four years of college under their belt and yet who knew so much more about the language, the mechanics, and the art of professional education than I did. Challenge accepted! I decided to press on to pursue a doctoral degree. I also learned I had much more to give than I previously realized and that I was much less needy than I believed. Kids enjoyed talking to me and they let me know it regularly with their hugs and laughter. In the process of feeding their growing curiosity, I found it was I who was being strengthened. Most importantly, I finally realized that in spite of my meager salary,

God had been taking care of me all along. In fact, He was simultaneously equipping me to handle both the work at my fingertips *and* the journey just ahead.

My attitude slowly shifted from an inside-the-cocoon perspective, to a point of view far above my prior limitations. Rather than working to fulfill only my own needs or giving to others with the expectation of receiving something in return, I made a conscious effort to invest my time and energy into meeting the needs of those I was in a position to respond to. I sought to pattern my behavior after the model that I witnessed daily as the children I worked with freely gave away their affection. Just like my "Clubhouse" kids, I learned to pause from time to time and receive what I needed along my journey, even if it came from unexpected sources. I learned to embrace *serendipity*—defined as the happenstance encounter of something either valuable or needed by mere chance and without actively seeking it!

To this day, I still view my career in education as a public service to my students and the city I worked in at the time. Because of this tiny shift in perspective, I learned to see that my students were also stocking me up with supplies for the difficulties in the years that followed. I was receiving love. Respect. Laughter. Open smiles, offered to me without any filter or self-consciousness. Honesty that pushed me, some days, to the point of tears. Even though I was still reporting to work in a basement every day, people had come into my life who truly needed me, while I, in turn, gained more confidence that I could open up creative avenues worthy for others to travel.

While I excelled in my graduate studies, I confess now that none of it was easy. I worked full-time as a teacher or administrator, went to school part-time, and always felt I was handling more than I could juggle. All the while, I struggled mightily not to completely drop all the balls I was expected to keep in the air at all times. I even taught myself to juggle a handball, a softball, and a basketball all at the same time— not only to entertain the kids at "Clubhouse" but for the sheer symbolism of the on-the-spot adjustments I was rapidly learning to make in life.

extended trajectory

Veering sharply to the shoulder
undercarriage pelted with stony debris
I am lifted upon a cloud of dust
wheels screaming, suddenly die
tractionless now above the snap snap of tall grass
until dredging a heavy scar across open field

I am bowled from the vehicle

Sliding, flipping
I see meadow
I see sky
I see possibilities
but my trajectory is unknown

Standing somehow

(I shouldn't be here)

several yards from fresh wreckage
I am bleeding, but whole
Skin abraded, ligaments stretched
but no bones have been broken this morning
and I'm not dead yet

I am left to find a way home
through the uncertainty that injury brings

I am dizzy;
one misdirection leads to yet another;

motion begets exploration;
the open field becomes a succession of moving targets;
possible destinations;
and I am the method of inquiry

I am inverted;
a body without organs
I am composed now of external vectors
and the possibility of multiple trajectories

I am extended along imaginary lines of inquiry
and I am on my way home
wherever I go.

12

death, then breathing

Funeral program designed by
my brother Chris, with some of
my father's illustrations.

~~AS CREATIVE AS I'VE~~ always been, I finally learned that
my superpowers were limited. Yes, I've always possessed the
imagination to improvise my way through life, but bodies can
break when you least expect them to. Just before my father's

body broke unexpectedly in the summer of 2002, I was a full-time college department director at Teachers College, Columbia University, *and* a part-time adjunct instructor at New York University. *And* working to complete my doctoral dissertation. *And* singing in a Grammy Award-winning choir during its heavy concert schedule. *And* taking it upon myself, as the eldest son, to officially push to have my father moved from a hospital with one of the worst reputations in Brooklyn to a better medical facility. I was behaving like Superman in the flesh, carrying every load placed on my shoulders and handling my business—until the day that summer when my business started handling me.

After my father's sudden death, I had to assist Ma in cleaning out 1260 Lincoln Place and executing my father's signed contract to sell our old home, whether we liked it or not. He was living alone when he fell into a diabetic coma so he had consulted none of us about the final details he'd agreed to in selling the house. My mother had moved out years before, unwilling and unable to continue to live under the same roof with him and after letting me know in advance (and seeking my blessing it seemed) of her plan to establish a home of her own where she could live in peace.

Naturally, I also took it upon myself to write my father's obituary, asserting my own power to reconstitute his dead body. I assembled the obituary from fragments of his life found after the fact: from my memory, an old resume, found letters, his job newsletters, newspaper articles, conversations with family and his friends, his grandmother's obituary, and from his mother's obituary and her final letter to her only child—carefully kept in a baby blue envelope for over 35 years and written on browning blue stationery.

OBITUARY

James Haywood Rolling, son of James H. & Eva B. Rolling, was born on September 28, 1938 in Brooklyn, NY. He succumbed to diabetes-related illness at St. Mary's Hospital in Brooklyn on July 8, 2002. He was 63 years old.

Mr. Rolling graduated from the School of Industrial Art (now known as the High School of Art & Design) in June of 1956. Over the next few years, he furthered his education at The Art Students League and at Pratt Institute's Night School. He went on to serve in the U.S. Army in the specialist function as Army Illustrator, stationed at Fort Dix, NJ from 1962 until he was honorably discharged in 1964.

Being a gifted fine artist, cartoonist, and graphic designer, in 1975 Mr. Rolling illustrated a children's book titled "Exploring Triangles: Paper-Folding Geometry," which was later translated into Chinese. Mr. Rolling was a Supervisor of Design and Display Lettering Manager from 1967 through 1977 for the Display Department of J.C. Penney, a major retailer. After 2 years of freelance design work at Barry Waldman Studios from 1977-1979, Mr. Rolling went to work for the Newspaper Advertising Bureau, Inc., from 1979-1991 representing 800 member newspapers. Mr. Rolling continued to increase his skills there, rising to the level of Senior Designer, developing and designing national campaigns to promote newspaper business. In 1991, he founded Jim Rolling Studios, serving as its Creative Director until his passing. Mr.

Rolling was the winner of several design awards and advertising honors during the 1970s and 1980s.

In 1983, Mr. Rolling won first place in the City Doubles Masters of the 6th Annual NYC (Budweiser) Paddleball Championship conducted by the NYC Department of Parks & Recreation, and was a frequent competitor in several other paddleball championships. Mr. Rolling was also an avid and masterful chess player, placing third in the Mount Olympus/Recreation Tournament in 1998. Because of his particular skills, Mr. Rolling was known to his daily chess buddies as "Nemesis." He also volunteered his time at community organizations, including conducting an art and writing workshop to young people at Vehicles, a life skills and career training organization located in East Harlem during the summer of 1998.

Extended surviving family include Steve Jordan, first cousin, L.I.; Sandra Joyce Graham & her sister, Janet Fay Mark, both second cousins of Brooklyn; Bernice Smith, great aunt, of CA; and a host of in-laws.

He is survived by his wife of 39 years, Sylvia J. (Lawrence) Rolling, whom he wed on July 2, 1963. They have four children: James Haywood Rolling, Jr. & his wife, Me'Shae of Manhattan; Dwayne Christopher Rolling & his wife, Toniann of Manhattan; Angela Evette Rolling of Brooklyn; and Mark Edward Rolling & his wife, Dorothy of Montclair, NJ. Two grandchildren and one on the way by Mark & Dorothy Rolling: Christina Carolyn and Christal Juanita Rolling.

He was preceded in death by his beloved paternal grandmother, Eva Haywood Rolling, in 1983, and by his dearly loved mother, Eva B. Rolling, in 1965.

*   *   *

My father was buried on July 15, 2002. By August 5, less than a month later, I was busily organizing the final supply orders needed in fulfilling my annual role as the art director of a week-long summer camp run by my church for New York City foster kids who had been severely abused. For nearly a decade prior to this, I always returned from the typical week of nonstop exertion at Royal Family Kids Camp physically and mentally exhausted. At the conclusion of each year's camp, it typically took me another full week just to recover from the strain on my lower back and legs alone, since I was usually on my feet or lugging supplies back and forth and back and forth across the campgrounds for at least 12 hours each day. Knowing the toll it would take on my body and mind, I had every reason to withdraw my commitment to volunteer again that particular summer—after all, my father had just died. But because I had already participated in preliminary trainings *before* my father fell ill, and knew my expertise was hard to replace, I was resolute in not wanting to back out or feel like I let anyone down.

I'm unsure when I first experienced having trouble breathing but I know I first *noticed* it at camp one night in my cabin after a packed day of running art centers and preparing backdrops and props for the ministry skits presented that afternoon. It started as creeping sense of claustrophobia. As the darkness in the room closed in on me and the one moonlit window in the room grew smaller, an unfamiliar panic began to rise in my chest, compelling me to get outside quickly so I could find my breath again. These intense, yet brief fore-warnings that I was losing control of my body would escalate within weeks into hours-long attacks where I couldn't control my breathing at all or fight off the feeling that there were metal bands tightening around my chest. My wife and I had originally joined the Brooklyn Tabernacle Choir ministry at our church at the end of 1997. During the years I sang with the tenor section, I participated in the recording of a number of albums, three of which won a string of GRAMMY Awards for Best Gospel Choir or Chorus Album in 1999, 2000, and 2002. One night at a 2002 choir concert in Staten Island as part of a September 11th memorial event, I ended up having to be carried off the stage and rushed away to a hospital emer-gency room in an ambulance. My senses were overwhelmed. I was literally driven to my knees by the amplified bass reverber-ations of heavily orchestrated soundtracks along with our 275 voices booming through the venue's giant outdoor speakers. Yet what I recall most vividly is that, at the time, it was quite evident to me that I was quietly having a heart attack.

After being monitored overnight and told that my heart was as strong as a bull's, I still continued to be plagued by debil-itating attacks. All told, I would be hospitalized three times within the space of the next two weeks before finally being diagnosed with the onset of a severe anxiety disorder. My nerves were so hyper-sensitized after returning home that I was forced to take baths instead of showers; I felt every single, individual droplet of water propelled from the shower head so keenly that the cumulative assault was too much for my internal wiring to bear. I went back to work as a Teachers College adminis-trator feeling broken open, with all my strength draining out in a gruesome trail of gore stretched behind me no matter how hard I struggled to hold myself together. Recognizing that I was not myself anymore, I confessed to my doctoral committee advisor, Dr. Graeme Sullivan, that I would not be able to finish my dissertation by the following year, as scheduled.

At home, each new anxiety attack left me feeling as if I was dying a slow death. All I could do in the midst of an attack was to weep on my bed to a few melodic worship albums by Terry Clark or Terry MacAlmon. They'd been gifted to me at the point of my deepest need—albums filled with songs I listened to over and over again, songs that slowly unratcheted the metal straps crushing my ribs, one notch at a time. Singing along with each song helped me to acknowledge and recalibrate the rhythm of my breathing.

In the remaining months of 2002, I sought the prayer of elders in my church who visited me until I was strong enough to venture outside on my own to see a professional therapist each week. Travel was difficult since I still did not yet have the anxiety under control. Motion, noise, or stress would trigger a panic attack. I had not even been able to grieve the loss of my father or process how it had changed me. Nevertheless, in spite of my doubts and malfunctions, Graeme told me he had every confidence I would finish my dissertation as originally planned. He explained that I had built up strong forward momentum and, just like a long-distance runner, the momentum of my studies would carry me across the finish line even as my legs were quaking beneath me. To prevent a premature collapse, Graeme asked me to trust my momentum and not lurch to a complete standstill.

While I had lost faith in my own body, I still trusted Graeme. So, I kept writing and, to my quiet surprise, I went on to earn my doctoral degree in education from Teachers College, Columbia University in 2003 as planned. Within that same year, I had also weaned myself off all anti-anxiety medication and began learning to control and measure each breath, while permitting the world—with its weights and burdens—to slide off my shoulders.

It would take YEARS before I could go through an anxious moment without the unwanted sensation of those metal bands beginning to tighten around my ribs again as I'd slip unknowingly into a ragged pattern of arrhythmic breathing. Looking back, my journey toward becoming a professional educator began with an unsteady first step—accepting a little part-time afterschool teaching job that no one else wanted. From where I stand now, I can clearly see that God had ordered my footsteps all along from there. I would not be where I am today if I had not first spent years struggling to find my way out of the windowless basement level of Hunter College Elementary School. Although I was initially a misfit as a teacher, I simply put one foot in front of the other when I could not see any progress and it seemed like it was taking forever to get anywhere. Even if I was still halfway inside my shell and could barely see what was on the road ahead of me, at least I was falling forward.

I finally came to understand that the reason I never fit in was because I did not know who I really was. I was not born ugly. I am not a birdbrain. I was never lost. The things that made me an outsider also made me an observer, a careful listener, a singer, an artist, a writer, and a teacher. I was used to noticing things that other people usually overlooked. I didn't hang out in the ghetto of my boyhood because I didn't belong in anyone's ghetto. Wherever I was, whenever I was wandering, God knew exactly where to find me. I came to realize that while the injuries I had collected over my life's story had left me with scars, the remedy I most needed was a reinterpretation—a retelling of my life's story in my own words rather than in the words of my father, of those that bullied me, or those that underestimated me. Today, I'm not just nicknamed "Professor"—I _am_ a full professor of art education at Syracuse University. I am a published author, a poet, a master of fine arts, a doctor of education, and, most importantly, a servant of God in my local community.

Today, I choose to write and draw for anyone within my reach, but especially for those who have been emotionally wounded. If you see yourself in my story, it is my gift to you. Who were you born to be? What has been your hardest struggle in life? What's that one trigger from your hardscrabble past that you keep getting your flesh caught in over and over again? Who's hurt you the most and where are you still bleeding? Now, what do you need to do to turn the page? Your storytelling makes all the difference. Your life is unique, and when you give it away, your present story also becomes the architecture for your sequels and your next great chapters. As the lead character, your story even opens the door for you to rename yourself in a world that has thrust all kinds of unwanted labels upon you.

When I was writing my father's obituary, I had to go through all his papers to make sure I told his final story accurately. Among my father's papers were handwritten notes about his family lineage through his paternal grandmother Eva, writings that were legally required for a property settlement about six months after her death. On January 11, 1983, my late father—in an effort to remember and connect the past to the future—wrote that besides Uncle Elmo:

> Eva Haywood [Rolling] had one other son, James Haywood Rolling. He and his wife, Eva [B.] (Hart) Rolling had one child, me, James H. Rolling Jr. My father, James senior died when I was very young and

my mother passed away in 1965. I reside at 1260 Lincoln Place, Brooklyn, N.Y. 11213.

In other words, I am actually James Haywood Rolling, III. I have been told that etiquette allows that since I am the third and last living James Haywood Rolling on the planet, I can drop the "Junior" from my surname. But I have elected not to do so. In spite of the ugliness unmasked throughout the tale, I want my father's story in the world since it will always be the preface for my own story and a cautionary tale for others. My father wanted to leave something behind as an artist. In my 1998 interview with him, I prompted him to share his hope for something not yet attained.

> Well, I'd like to do work good enough for people to admire…for it to please people…for it to kind of make them think when they see what I do, to inspire them to be good at what they do. Which is something I realize that really talented people do…they don't just do for themselves. They kind of try to inspire other people, lead other people…and give them something to carry on. Because we're not all going to be here… we're only here for a certain amount of time. So hopefully, for your life to have been worth something, you want to create something that people remember… even if it's your children or whomever.

My father very much wanted to leave something behind and I'm part of what was left. At the time he spoke these words he also confessed that he'd been "kind of in a tunnel, but I see light ahead." Although he never lived to see it, I hope this book is a source of that light and a part of his creative legacy that will do some long-lasting good.

Remnants

One year after sudden illness
after the collapse
of safe and familiar routine
and the onset of new attacks
even after your death

eight months after three hospitalizations
and debates with my own mortality
a conversation continues
within my chest cavity
metallic bands ratcheted against each rib

seven months after the first tears burst
unexpectedly outpouring
from a bowl of insecurity
carefully shaped by your hand
a memorial to my childhood

the floating shards of your legacy
remain in my bloodstream
broken pottery from your own childhood's end
your junk piles
and closet collections
left as my inheritance

sickled shards are still settling in
my joints distended and organs congealed
a crisis of distorted blood cells
remnants
after the fall

when quietly
your life of clay
spiraled to the kitchen floor
broken body chemistry
soaked in its own urine

braced against an unforgiving radiator

EPILOGUE
drawing superheroes on blank pages

A photographic self-portrait, reflected in
a restroom mirror at The Cooper Union.

CREATIVITY MATTERS. STORY MATTERS. As I conclude
this memoir, first things first. I'm an eldest sibling. I'm also a
teacher. In other words, it's both my natural and professional
inclination to instruct and feel responsible for others under
my influence. So, I offer you this challenge. Make something
from nothing. From a blank canvas. From an empty page.
Through the open frame of your camera lens. Think of it this
way. Making something from nothing starts with hunting
and gathering. Start with what you have directly at hand and

who you already are. **Gather yourself first.** What are you capable of that no one ever gets to see? What are you so interested in that it absorbs your free time and attention? **Now, hunt through the circumstances of your life and gather what's already at hand.** What purpose does it serve and how can it be re-purposed to fulfill a different need? Disassemble it and put it together differently or in a new location or with new connectors, just like you did when you first played with wooden blocks in kindergarten. Avengers assemble!

*   *   *

In this epilogue to "Growing Up Ugly," I've arrived at the place where I first began my journey as an artist. I've always loved superheroes from the time I first encountered them in my father's art studio. I've always seen a parallel between teaching oneself to master newly emerging superpowers and teaching myself to master my own creative powers. In fact, I've always viewed my creativity as a collection of superpowers. Drawing upon my familiarity with comic book illustration and inking, I once developed a Sunday Bible Hour lesson that included the following memory verse poster I drew to aid each student's visualization of the power of creative agency to shape a life.

The ensuing account is a useful tale about how we can rewrite the story of our lives with each act of creation. Artists know this already, both innately and through their personal practices, but it isn't yet common knowledge although it should be. At the end of the 2004-05 school year, my final year working fulltime as an elementary school art teacher, I proposed the "Who I Am" storytelling project to take place during that trimester's Integrated Projects Week (IPW) at The School. In this project-based learning engagement, family artifacts, heirlooms, and personal knowledge were to serve as the inspiration for art-making, children's research, and the performance of self-image and family identity. Another teacher assisted me. The students who chose to participate in the "Who I Am" project were first required to bring home a letter introducing the notion of young children researching their own family stories and transforming meaningful personal knowledge and family heirlooms into creative works.

A poster visualizing the superpower
of creativity to reshape a life.

To inaugurate the "Who I Am" project, I gathered the seven participating students into an empty classroom. We sat down on a rug in a storytelling circle with a few learning objects on hand. First, I introduced *1260 Lincoln Place*, a mixed-media representation of my experience of the home I grew up in, constructed ten years prior to this particular art classroom project. It incorporates a life-sized and three-dimensional self-portrait, along with a portrait of my younger brother Chris, both of us visible in through the bedroom window.

Each brick on the face of the exterior wall was handcrafted and placed askew; the figures of my brother and I were molded out of soil and clay. The careful modeling of the facial features was colored with layer upon layer of a variety of oil pastels. The shirts worn by the two figures were cut from the rags of shirts we actually wore as children. The working set of venetian blinds were actually taken from my old bedroom window and installed into the artwork. The print of the youngster playing baseball was a one-generation old heirloom passed down to us; it was once hung on my father's bedroom wall when he himself was a boy and was valuable for no other reason. The entire piece was too heavy to be physically passed around the storytelling circle as an object, so my students were invited to step forward and touch the bricks and faces depicted in the artwork, as well as to raise and lower the blinds.

1260 Lincoln Place, a mixed-media self-portrait representing the home I grew up in.

This first learning object was then juxtaposed with some very old photographs that I subsequently passed around which belonged to the family albums of my friend Pam. I first met Dr. Pamela Harris Lawton when we were both students of art education in the same doctoral program at Teachers College, Columbia University. She is currently a member of the faculty at the Maryland Institute College of Art (MICA). Like me, Pam is also a studio artist and arts-based researcher. Pam has described her effort to condense family stories, records and photographs into visual and verbal artifacts of her creative lineage that are accessible and easy to read. In her words: "I wanted to create visual documents that could be circulated, used to teach family history to the young, and yet be so aesthetically pleasing that instead of being filed safely away in a trunk, drawer or closet, they could be displayed as works of art in the homes of family members where inquisitive young minds and eyes could seek them out and ask questions."

As I was conceiving the "Who I Am" project, I recalled viewing one such work of art exhibited by Pam several years prior at Teachers College, a story based upon her rescue of a family heirloom—a compact folding portable desk invented in the early 1940s by one of her recent ancestors, an accomplished architectural modelmaker and dollhouse designer named James W. Butcher. The original photographs and copies of newspaper articles that Pam was kind enough to send me included photos of the heirloom in disrepair upon initial discovery and retrieval from some attic, basement, or closet. The portable desk was then photographed once again after the loving act of re-search, restoration, and storytelling curated by Pam as she transformed the once-forgotten heirloom into a work of art. Regarding the portable desk and her reclamation of the legacy of her "Papa Will" (as Mr. Butcher was affectionately called among family members), Pam wrote: "Papa Will used wallpaper to decorate the sides of his desks. I peeled off the wallpaper and in place of its collaged prints and photocopies of photos and documents telling the story of Papa Will's life on the outside panels of the desk. And then because he was so involved in making things by hand, I had the idea of sculpting in clay a replica of his hands in the act of sketching ideas for future woodworking projects—in effect putting him into the piece."

After viewing both my artwork and Pam's artwork one right after the other and handling both sets of learning objects with care, the children in the storytelling circle were asked to reflect on their own life stories to make some connections of their own. What heirloom from their home would they each like to ask permission from their parents to bring to class and transform into a creative work? My students considered the possibilities with much enthusiasm; each child was given a sketchbook and asked to mark out some preliminary ideas for their projects as they came to mind. Creativity is a super-power. They would figure it out on their own.

Nyasa, one of my third-grade students, discovered her own superpower to speak life into the story of her great grandmother's immigration to the United States from the Caribbean island of Barbados, an essential part of the tale of family origins leading to her own childhood in the present-day United States. The opportunity to make art in her elementary school classroom was stimulated with a simple and precious family heirloom—a jar of sand carried away from the beaches of Barbados when her great grandmother just before she immigrated to these shores. As she mulled through the many possible creative outcomes, Nyasa found a connection that made sense to her, a story she knew that was worth telling through a series of clay figurines, a story of the passage of time and the passing down of cherished meaning from one generation to the next. I asked all my students to write about the significance of the idea revisited through their art-making. Nyasa told this story:

> My great grandmother came to this country with her two children and a jar of sand with her from the beach. She brought the sand with her as a reminder of Barbados. The sand is a piece of her country [and] it also represents if we can't be in Barbados, it will be with us...I began with the sand and thought about what I was going to do. I got the idea of making a timeline to show how the sand got passed down the family tree...I got the idea of using clay people to symbolize my family, giving the sand to one another. I put my great grandmother and my grandmother in the first box, my grandmother and mother in the second box and my mother and me in the third box...I got the idea of making it three-dimensional because I thought it would be weird if it was on paper. I also got the idea of how I want to tell the story.

Nyasa's timeline of genealogical inheritance.

Nyasa's homeroom class had been studying timelines and family trees during the recent school year. As her art teacher, I had not been studying these things in the school's art room and any suggestions I might have offered drawn from my own personal knowledge would likely have led Nyasa in other directions. However, for the sake of the children's research, I let my students initiate their own directions and develop their own sense of the meaning of the story they wished to tell about themselves. I was to be on hand primarily to facilitate their creations.

My fourth-grade student, Dustin, discovered his own superpower to make the invisible visible as he saw his great-grandmother on his father's side for the very first time. Dustin's personal family artifact was a green beret that first belonged to his great-grandmother, was passed down to his father, and then given to Dustin. According to Dustin, his great-grandmother Adda Bozeman spoke at military academies during the Vietnam War era and was an advocate in favor of the effectiveness of human intelligence over too great a reliance upon satellite surveillance in the practice of international espionage. The green beret was apparently a gift to Dr. Bozeman in connection with one of these speeches about best practices in spycraft. This was all that Dustin knew. He told me he had never seen a photograph of his great-grandmother before.

I proceeded to help Dustin do a quick online search for his great-grandmother's name and we found out that she had been a Professor of International Relations at Sarah Lawrence College. Moreover, we discovered that the Sarah Lawrence College Archives had photographs of Dr. Bozeman in her role as an educator. I made an urgent request for digital copies of these photos on behalf of Dustin so that he could incorporate them into his project within the week. Given the tight timeline, it was to our delight that our request was granted.

For Dustin, receiving photographs of a family member he had never met or seen was like uncovering buried treasure. His parents had never before seen these particular photos either, so Dustin was able to forward the images home as a gift, to his father especially.

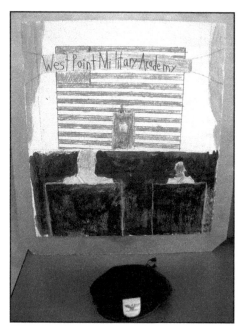

Dustin's beret and painting of his great-grandmother teaching at West Point.

Tal, one of my third-graders, was also a student in my regular-day art classroom twice a week. He had elected to sign up for my afterschool portrait-making class as well as the additional week-long "Who I Am" IPW offering. Tal discovered his own superpower to make meaning with nothing but his bare hands and a pencil. In the following correspondence shared with me by Tal's mother, a research psychiatrist at a

New York City hospital at the time, she introduces her son as an emerging creative identity:

> I have a wonderful son named Tal (age 9) who has many talents. However, fine motor control and visual perception were not two of them. As a child, he never drew—ever. It was unclear whether this was due to lack of interest, lack of skill, or some combination of the two. His passion was baseball, and you didn't need to draw to play shortstop. As a result, when he told me one day that his only complaint with his new school was that he did not have enough art time I was startled. Even more startling was when he signed up for "Master Portrait Drawing" as an afterschool class. He chose this class even though it required attendance twice a week for 2-hour sessions each, and it prevented him from playing afterschool basketball with his best friend. I kept my mouth shut as he filled out the after-school form, but I wondered if he would even last one week. In fact, he lasted all semester, he chose an extra week of art at the end of the school year, and he lamented the fact that his teacher was moving away and would not be at school the following year. For the first time in his life, Tal liked drawing and looked forward to art class.

Why would a self-described sports enthusiast who brought his baseball glove to school each day and expressed almost no interest in art before the third grade take a path so seemingly at odds with his previous journey? It was because, through my art class, Tal had tapped into his powers as a creative superhero and found it to be good thing. Tal's mother followed her son's development closely that school year and noticed several things that were out of the ordinary for him, things that appeared to her trained eyes to be a direct consequence of tapping into creative ways of knowing and doing that were entirely new to him.

The first thing I noticed as Tal worked week after week on his family portraits was that he began to notice visual details in the external world. Historically, this was a child who struggled to discern E from F or to find something in the refrigerator right in front of him...The second thing I noticed was his increasing ability to see both the forest and the trees. Historically, Tal had a tendency toward tunnel-vision: when he noticed a detail, he saw nothing else. He could get caught on one word in a sentence and miss the overall meaning. However, in art class, Tal was learning how to draw his brother's face, which required that he draw his brother's two eyes, nose, mouth and teeth all in the right proportion to each other. Then, he drew his mother's eyes in his mother's face, his father's ears on his father's head, etc. To make his family portraits look like his family, Tal had to move back and forth between the forest (i.e., the overall effect) and the trees (i.e., the specific facial features). I began to notice his increasing ability to do this not only with his drawing but with his thinking as well. Whether drawing taught him to do this or whether he was ready to do this and drawing was a way to practice combining the part with the whole, I don't know. However, the growth in his conceptual flexibility was quite dramatic.

Beyond all of these things, Tal found an ability to tell new stories, filling in the gaps of his personal knowledge as he figured out his own creative identity. Tal's heirloom for the "Who I Am" project was the book from which his name was taken, titled *TAL, His Marvelous Adventures with Noom-Zor-Noom* (1929), by author Paul Fenimore Cooper, the great-grandson of the renowned early American novelist James Fenimore Cooper. Tal did not want to permanently install this book into a work of art so he instead chose to make a small bookshelf made out of some thick corrugated cardboard we had tucked away in one of the art studio storage closets. Tal writes about his name, his family and his "being here" in the following excerpt of his in-class writing:

> When my mom was a kid her third grade teacher read her the book "Tal," she thought it was such a great and mysterious book. The only other person my mom knew who read the book outside of her class was her sister Lisa who had the same teacher when she was in third grade. Years later my mom met my dad. He also knew the book "Tal" because his uncle [Paul Fenimore Cooper] wrote the book. One of the earliest presents from my dad to my mom was the book "Tal"! My dad went to an out-of-print book shop, and found the book "Tal" and he gave it to my mom. They decided upon Tal as my name because they both loved the book. But in the book the boy named Tal actually had blond hair and blue eyes. I have dark hair and brown eyes.

The book was not the only object in Tal's assembly of story components—he also added several other examples of his identity in this telling. Incorporated into his bookshelf,

Tal included a baseball; a second heirloom, his baseball glove, which first belonged to his father and was passed on to Tal; a clay jaguar, representing Tal's favorite animal, made specifically for placement within the installation; a rolled paper "chessboard" that was hand-ruled and hand-inked by Tal, a replication of the soft vinyl chessboards favored by the school-sponsored chess program he participated in; a copy of the front cover end paper of the book written by his father's uncle, so richly inked by the book's illustrator, Ruth Reeves, that Tal glued onto the lower shelf of his installation; other poetry and narratives written for the occasion; and a family photograph of Tal, his little brother and parents, glued to a small picture frame constructed by Tal, and set atop the completed bookshelf.

Tal's bookshelf of family artifacts.

* * *

I have shared these stories with you in this final chapter in order to prepare you for a question. What is your superpower? You probably already know what it is. It's that thing you love to work at and perfect when no one else is watching. It's that thing you have a gift for. It's that thing you would do even if no one paid you. **Now, what is holding you back from developing your superpowers?** For me, it was simply fear. Back in May of 1990, I transcribed the following words in my prayer journal, instructions which came to me after a time of prayer and seeking direction from God.

> **Become a writer.**
> **Draw and paint the word of God for it is the world's window to eternity.**
> **Use your skills primarily for the writing of books**
> **to broadcast and proclaim my Name and my nature**
> **to young and to old at home and abroad.**

But the path toward living in and walking out my superpower has not been straightforward. I confess I've gotten lost along the way. At times I've suffered from analysis paralysis. At times I've doubted myself. At times I was distracted. At times I was trapped in my own bad habits and procrastination. At times my full-time teaching job and service commitments were too enormous to manage. Some of those times were years long.

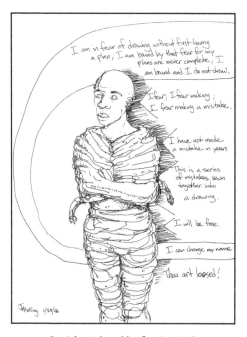

Straight-jacketed by fear in 2006.

At this point, nearly 30 years since I first documented those words, I have published several books as a professor of the arts in education and arts-based research. I've even published a children's book, with more to come in the next few years. I have published an inspirational book featuring my testimony of faith. But this particular book, "Growing Up Ugly," finally being published over 10 years after I first began writing it, is the first book I am releasing through my own publishing company, *Simple Word Publications*. I also believe it is the first book that begins to fulfill the instructions above. In my life, I have learned that the essential nature of God is that of a creator. God's love creates new life. God's mercy creates redemption and new opportunities.

God's vision creates order from chaos. I'm sure God saw who I could be and what I could be doing long before I did. This is why God found me. So I could learn to grow beyond my limits. So I could learn to fly. That's what I now proclaim. And, through this writing, I'm now sharing this same proclamation: Your creativity is the power to save and rewrite lives, starting with your own. I've already written the next books I'll be publishing. What's next for you? Here are some ideas.

Make a book from nothing.

Make a business from nothing.

Make a career change from nothing.

Make a living from nothing but your total investment.

Remember, some people are misinterpreted as nothing much, when all they are is overlooked, underestimated, or undiscovered—held out of sight, on the margins of consideration, or forgotten over time. Similarly, something that appears at first to be nothing much can suddenly be reinterpreted as something of great value. All it needs is a makeover, flipping the script in a way that changes its goals, offers unexpected purpose, or raises it from dysfunction. Here's what it takes:

To make something from nothing requires a willingness to play with both commitment and abandon, and to feel a little lost—a commitment to wander off road and try a new route to Point B…to knock down the wall and start over from scratch…to look under the fallen log just to see what's crawled under there…to retrace your steps while walking backwards in order to see what you'd missed the first time around.

To make something from nothing will demand that you master practices and techniques you'd never before tested, new platforms that will motivate you to learn a great deal more than before.

To make something from nothing begins with a self-guided tour of new knowledge content—educating yourself to tinker and tool around until you arrive at a new position of expertise in the world.

To make something from nothing is the most fundamental creative act—the first level of making upon which all other achievements are built.

To make something from nothing requires that we tear old structures down to the basement level and start over again with the same old wooden blocks we first learned how to assemble in kindergarten.

So, make a new episode. What story will you tell? Collect the building blocks of the story from the carpet of your memory. Write each word of your new chapter with purpose. Raise up each wall. There is a reason why your story feels different from everyone else's. You can tell it. Rap it. Write it. Sing it. All of the above. But it's *yours* to communicate like no one else can. For those who are young, I can tell you that life will get better. For those who are older, I'm happy to report that life goes on, even when you think it's too late or you've taken an unplanned turn and feel totally lost. Take a step forward, right now, and you'll suddenly have momentum and new direction no matter how long you've stood still.

If you're smart, don't play dumb. If you care deeply, don't waste time pretending that you don't. If you like to read, feed on as many books as you please. And if you need to wear glasses to sharpen your vision, take time to fix your eyes on the people and the principles that others choose to overlook. Study those things. If you want to live an outstanding life, the easiest way to stand out is by getting out of your own way first. Never settle for less when you can make something valuable from scratch.

Now, feel free. Take a deep breath.

Breathe in. Live an important life.

Breathe out. Imagine the best.

Breathe in. Bend boundary lines and erase old borders.

Breathe out. Give your art away.

Breathe in. Defy other people's low expectations.

Breathe out. Rise to meet someone else's need.

*   *   *

When I was still learning to teach, I had a second grade student who needed to slip out of his chair at odd intervals in the middle of a class discussion, grab on tightly to my waist, my hand, or my leg, perhaps even wrapping his legs around me, and squeeze as if his life depended on it. All the while he'd look me straight in the eye waiting for my discomfort level rise to a place where I had to, with some embarrassment, peel him off of my person. Nor could he keep his hands off the bodies of the children he considered to be his friends. He regularly complained of people being against him, and often fell into precipitous tantrums. His desperate grasping is entirely understandable. He was in therapy. His parents had separated. He had a sunken chest which ultimately required some surgery. He also had great difficulty controlling his emotions. In a writing and drawing class I used to teach, he once wrote of and depicted a monster child who was "born wrong." The monster in his story can't contain his anger, grows up to hurt people and animals, and is periodically put out of his misery by a headbutt from heroic Captain Blockhead. I've always believed the monster and Captain Blockhead were actually the same boy, learning to exercise his superpower of self-control.

When I was still learning to draw, I would use the large paper layout pads in my father's art studio to tell stories of secret underground bases and intergalactic battles among spaceships, each one filled with as many chambers as an ant colony, each chamber geared for a different purpose. I still like telling stories—stories, like this one, about growing up ugly but finally learning that what I thought was ugliness was really just my way of coping with injury.

People used to say I daydreamed too much, as if it was a bad habit. But my daydreams were windows, portals to all kinds of *what-ifs* and *why-nots* and distant worlds that give birth to superheroes. More than once, I made a new start that'd begun as no more than a daydream. It has not been an easy composition, but my latest sketches have been liberating. I'm already working on my next chapter. Now it's time to figure out your own way to what comes next. Black lives matter because our lives tell a story that too many Americans have ignored for too long, and no one's story should ever be ignored. But just as importantly, *your* life matters, whoever you are and wherever you come from. Each paragraph you add to the great human storybook is the stuff new endings are made of. I'm still a superhero. So are you.

Manifesto

I am an artist
this is who I am
making something from nothing
images and words flung
on empty pages
like God's first experiment
still expanding
searching out
the next big bang
revising
our communal poem

CPSIA information can be obtained
at www.ICGtesting.com
Printed in the USA
BVHW031825051121
620911BV00005B/231